STARTING OUT IN
SHARES
THE ASX WAY

STARTING OUT IN
SHARES
THE ASX WAY

THIRD EDITION

Wrightbooks
A Wiley Brand

This edition first published in 2015 by Wrightbooks, an imprint of John Wiley & Sons Australia, Ltd

42 McDougall St, Milton Qld 4064
Office also in Melbourne

Typeset in 11.3/14pt ITC Berkeley Oldstyle Std by Aptara, India

© ASX Operations Pty Ltd 2015

The moral rights of the author have been asserted

National Library of Australia Cataloguing-in-Publication data:

Creator:	Australian Securities Exchange, author.
Title:	Starting Out in Shares the ASX Way / Australian Securities Exchange.
Edition:	3rd edition.
ISBN:	9780730315667 (pbk.)
	9780730315674 (ebook)
Notes:	Includes index.
Subjects:	Australian Securities Exchange.
	Stocks—Australia.
	Investments—Australia.
Dewey Number:	332.63220994

Cover design by Wiley

Cover images by ASX Limited. Used with permission.

Printed in Singapore by C.O.S. Printers Pte Ltd

10 9 8 7 6 5 4 3 2 1

Disclaimer
The material in this publication is of the nature of general comment only, and does not represent professional advice. It is not intended to provide specific guidance for particular circumstances and it should not be relied on as the basis for any decision to take action or not take action on any matter which it covers. Readers should obtain professional advice where appropriate, before making any such decision. To the maximum extent permitted by law, the author and publisher disclaim all responsibility and liability to any person, arising directly or indirectly from any person taking or not taking action based on the information in this publication.

Contents

Introduction

These days more people than ever before have an interest in the sharemarket. It is easier and cheaper to buy and sell shares, there is more information about the market and most of us have a stake in the performance of the market through our superannuation funds.

So, if you are reading this introduction, you too have probably decided that you want to know more about investing.

But where to start?

Starting Out in Shares the ASX Way is a good place to start because for more than 30 years the Australian Securities Exchange (ASX) has been educating people starting out in the world of investing.

You may not know:

¤ what a share is

¤ how the sharemarket operates

¤ how to buy and sell

¤ what you need to have ready before you get in touch with a stockbroker.

We will walk you through all this and a lot more as well.

People often get a bit overwhelmed about investing in the sharemarket because, for many, it is unfamiliar territory with unfamiliar language. We will try to avoid jargon as much as possible, but we will explain terms to you that you are likely to encounter when you step into the world of investing.

Part I of the book intends to get you thinking about why you want to invest, what your objectives are and the various choices you have. We go into detail about how to buy and sell shares and how the market operates. In Part II we get into the nitty-gritty of having a balanced portfolio and how to set up an investment strategy.

* * *

By the end of the book we hope you have a good overview of the basics of investing and can confidently take your next steps in your investment journey.

PART I
The basics of the sharemarket

Starting Out in Shares the ASX Way aims to explain what shares are and how to buy and sell them. The book is targeted at people who are new to share investment. Part I of the book compares the benefits of shares over other investments, how the sharemarket works and how to set yourself up for share investment.

CHAPTER 1

Getting ready to invest

When you turn your mind to the prospect of investing in the sharemarket there are a lot of different aspects to consider. Why do you want to invest in the market? What are your investment goals? Consider whether your objectives are sound and realistic and how you are going to achieve them. This leads to thinking about mapping out your investment strategy. Then there are the practicalities of actually investing—that is, of *doing* it.

Saving versus investing

Saving involves setting money aside in a safe place in the hope that you will accumulate an amount sufficient to cover your future financial requirements. You can improve your chances of success by reducing your living expenses and lowering your lifestyle expectations. People with a strong savings mentality are good at this. Following this strategy means that your money may be safe as there is little chance of losing it. However, there is little you can do to protect its buying power from the debilitating effect of inflation.

Investing, on the other hand, makes your money work for you. Investors look for opportunities to put their money to use so that it may grow and create greater wealth for them. They assess alternative investment opportunities in terms of the potential risk involved, weighing them against the potential return to be made from the investment.

Strategies that take both inflation and taxation into account will improve your success as an investor, as will diversifying your risk across a range of investments.

What is your current life situation?

Your own personal circumstances, responsibilities and obligations will be major factors in determining your ability to invest and what you hope to achieve. You should consider the following:

¤ *Age and expected time remaining before retirement*—how much time do you have to achieve your goals?

¤ *Occupation and employment status*—do you have job security and a reliable income, or are you self-employed or a pensioner?

¤ *Spouse's age, occupation and retirement plans*—have you included your spouse's or partner's situation in your planning?

¤ *Family and dependants*—do you want to provide for your children's education, for example, or other needs?

¤ *Plans for your family home*—do you own your family home and will you sell it when you retire? Will you buy another home?

¤ *Standard of living*—what are your standard of living expectations, including holidays, entertainment and luxury items?

¤ *Estate planning*—have you planned for any future distribution of your wealth?

¤ *Personal control*—how much control do you like to have in managing your financial situation?

◻ *Insurance*—are you adequately protected against risks to your property, possessions, income and wellbeing? It is important to insure your assets against loss. If you are earning an income, you are your most valuable asset and it is important to consider insuring your income against loss through illness, accidents or disability.

Current financial position

It is important to take stock of your current financial position, as it will affect your ability to raise funds for immediate investment. Also, your stockbroker or adviser will require information about your current position in order to provide you with suitable investment advice.

There are some excellent online calculators on the MoneySmart website (www.moneysmart.gov.au). MoneySmart is an initiative of the Australian Securities and Investments Commission (ASIC), which provides a wealth of general financial resources beyond investing in the sharemarket.

Goals

Take a moment to reflect on your goals:

◻ How much money should I invest?

◻ Where should I invest—the sharemarket, cash or property?

Goal setting means thinking about what is important in the medium to long term, how much those goals will cost and how you plan to afford them.

How much money do you have to invest?

The amount of capital you have available for immediate investment will include the value of your current investments, any surplus after-tax income and, potentially, the value of some of your general assets if you are prepared to sell or borrow against them.

Risk—what it means to me

Investment risk refers to both the possibility of loss and uncertainty about future conditions.

Your attitude towards risk will affect how much money you make available for investment and how you invest it. To determine your risk profile, you should consider the following questions:

¤ How comfortable are you with risk and not being able to control some aspects of investment?

¤ Are you prepared to expose some of your money to higher risk for the opportunity of making higher returns, or are you more comfortable with low-risk, low-return investments?

¤ How reliable is your income and are your budgeted expenses realistic?

¤ Do you have a large amount of debt?

Time frame—income and capital growth

Timing is another factor in determining your investment objectives. If you need funds to achieve short-term goals, you should invest in areas that are more likely to perform earlier rather than later. Alternatively, you may wish to grow your investments over the long term.

Requirements regarding timing, as well as your current lifestyle needs, will determine the returns you should seek from your investments.

When considering how timing may affect your investment objectives, ask yourself whether you require:

¤ a return in the form of income to support your current lifestyle

¤ a return in the form of capital growth to increase your wealth over time

¤ a combination of income and capital growth.

Diversification

A popular saying is 'don't put all your eggs in one basket'. It can apply to many things, but it applies particularly well to investing in the sharemarket and the need for diversification.

Markets move in cycles. Some investors fall into the trap of putting all their money into one asset class—usually when it is at its peak—and then watch as another asset class takes off without them (an asset class is an investment area such as shares or property). The sharemarket is one asset class you can use to diversify your portfolio.

There is much debate as to how many stocks you should invest in to achieve prudent diversification, and this is something you need to consider and discuss with your adviser if you have one. Some advisers recommend having more than 20 stocks; others suggest that with a wary eye to correlation you can create a reasonably diversified and balanced portfolio with 10 or 12 stocks.

Are you ready to start investing in shares?

Once you have assessed your current financial situation and developed your future plans, you should be ready to start looking at different investment strategies and working out which strategies best suit your needs and objectives.

So if you're ready, let's get started!

CHAPTER 2

What is a share and what is the sharemarket?

A share is simply part-ownership of a business. A company can raise money to finance its business by 'going public'. Going public means being listed on a stock exchange and issuing shares to investors. When you buy shares in a company, you own part of that company.

The money that a company raises in the sharemarket is called 'equity capital'. Unlike debt capital, which is borrowed money, equity capital does not need to be repaid as it represents continuous ownership of the company.

As a shareholder you have certain rights and obligations, and you also share in the risks associated with the fortunes of that company.

Shares in a listed company can be sold to other investors on the sharemarket. In this way, you can realise capital gains if the share price has risen—in other words, you can make a profit by selling the shares for more than you paid for them. As a shareholder you may benefit by receiving income in the form of cash distributions, called 'dividends'.

As a part-owner in the business you may be entitled to vote on the direction of the company, the election of new company directors or other matters.

All shareholders should be aware that the value of a share can fall to zero. In the case of a company going broke and being wound up, shareholders rank close to last in the list of people who can claim money from the sale of the company's assets.

What is the sharemarket?

There are a number of approved securities exchanges in Australia, the largest of which is the Australian Securities Exchange (ASX), which has more than 2000 companies on its Official List.

The sharemarket may be thought of in terms of its two separate market functions: the primary market and the secondary market.

The primary market—where it starts

If a company wants to set up a new business or expand its existing business it can raise the money (capital) it needs by issuing new shares to investors. The investors who invest money by buying these shares become shareholders in the company.

Companies that want to issue shares on the sharemarket must first be listed on an approved securities exchange. Most get listed on the ASX. The requirements for listing include being large enough to achieve a market in its shares and agreeing to abide by the ASX Listing Rules. These rules require listed companies to inform the sharemarket of any activities that may affect the price of the shares on the market and to report company profits and other specified financial information.

Many people invest in the sharemarket by participating in the initial public offering (IPO) of shares made by a company listing on the ASX. Access to public floats can vary considerably depending on the size of the float, how many shares are being made available, whether a large portion is allocated to institutional clients or retail investors, and of course whether there is a demand for shares in the company.

The terms 'IPO', 'float', 'listing' and 'going public' are often used interchangeably.

The secondary market—where people buy and sell shares

After a company has completed its float and issued shares to investors, the shares can be sold to other investors on the sharemarket. This is referred to as the secondary market.

Share trading takes place through the agency of stockbrokers who enter buy and sell orders on behalf of investors.

The price of the shares is determined by the forces of supply and demand, with investors deciding what they will pay for shares in individual companies or what they will accept for shares they already own. The growth and profitability of the companies, alongside other external factors, influence these decisions.

*   *   *

Now that you have an understanding of the market itself and the difference between the primary and secondary market, it is time to talk about your choices when it comes to investing.

CHAPTER 3

The main investment areas:
cash, fixed interest, property, shares

This chapter contains general factual information on the main investment areas and does not constitute financial advice. You should seek independent advice from an Australian Financial Services (AFS) licensee prior to making any investment decisions.

Financial advisers are often asked, 'Where is the best place to invest my money?' In asking such a question, their clients might be hoping to be told that there is one sure bet—for example, that shares are better than interest-paying investments or that property is the best method of increasing wealth. Of course, depending on your financial goals and objectives, one particular form of investment may be better than another for you at a particular point in your life. However, it is never advisable to have all your eggs in one basket. Even the so-called safe investments such as bank savings accounts involve an element of risk—most notably the risk of the value being eroded by inflation.

In general terms, there are four main types of investment, often referred to as asset classes:

- *Cash*—where you invest money in a building society, bank or other financial institution. Investment options include cash management accounts, and a major benefit of this investment type is liquidity.

- *Fixed interest*—where you invest in short- or long-term interest rate products that provide a steady income stream. Investment options include bonds, deposits, bank bills and various other types of securities. For more information on fixed-interest products, go to the ASX website: www.asx.com.au.

- *Property*—where you invest in residential, rural, industrial or commercial property. Depending on your retirement plans and financial objectives, your home may be included in this investment class.

- *Shares*—where you invest in companies listed on the ASX and other stock exchanges.

Investment considerations

Evaluating investment opportunities is easiest if you use a standard set of criteria to measure and compare them. Each investment should be evaluated in the context of your goals and objectives and then the following characteristics (among others) should be considered:

- return on investment

- capital and income security (or risk)

- ease of investment

- liquidity and other market conditions

- minimum investment

- costs

- time frame for performance

- choice and ability to diversify

- taxation.

Return on investment

Return on investment is usually in the form of income (a payment you receive from your investment) or capital growth (where the value of your investment increases over time). Some investments, such as shares or property, may provide both.

Income

Investment income includes amounts such as interest on bank accounts, dividends from shares, rent from a property and distributions from a trust. As well as the amount of income you are likely to receive, you should consider the likely frequency of the payments and the potential for any increases or bonuses. As income from investments is usually subject to income tax at your marginal tax rate, you should always take the income provided after tax into account. Some forms of investment income, such as fully franked dividends, may provide some investors with tax benefits; however, we recommend that you obtain your own taxation advice from a professional adviser before making any investment decisions.

Capital growth

Returns from capital growth can only be realised when you sell an investment for more than the purchase price. The main benefit of capital growth is that it protects you against inflation. Capital growth may occur through rising share and unit trust prices on the sharemarket, increased values in the property market, and/or profit on fixed-interest securities if sold before maturity. Realised capital growth from investments is usually subject to capital gains tax.

Visit the website of the Australian Taxation Office (www.ato.gov.au) for up-to-date information on tax matters.

Capital and income security

How secure is your investment capital? Is it possible your investment will be worth less when you wish to sell it? Will you be able to sell it at all if there is a shortage of buyers or if the financial institution you have invested in defaults? By answering these questions you are identifying your risk of capital loss.

In addition to your capital, how secure is the income from your investment? For example, in the case of an investment property, will there always be a tenant to pay rent? This is an important consideration if you are relying on investment income to supplement your income from other sources or to support your lifestyle. In addition, unreliable or fluctuating income may affect the sale price or capital gain of your investment.

When considering capital and income security, it is important to take into account price volatility and the risk/reward equation.

Volatility

Volatility refers to the general tendency of the price of an investment to fluctuate as buyers and sellers enter and leave the market.

Short-term price fluctuations matter less when you invest for the long term and when the price is expected to rise overall during the period of investment. Whereas a three-year investment is usually considered to be short term, a long-term investment can be seven years or more.

If you sold your house on seven different days, you would get a different price each day. In the short term, the sharemarket really isn't all that different.

The risk/return equation

The risk/return equation balances the possible risk (of loss) against the possible return (or profit) of an investment.

You should only invest as much in high-risk investments as you are prepared to lose. For example, 'safe' or low-risk investments such as bank accounts often pay lower rates of interest or offer lower returns, while high-risk investments often provide an opportunity for higher rates of return.

Ease of investment

Ease of investment is another important consideration when deciding which asset class to invest in. Look at how hard it is to enter the asset class and what processes you need to go through when you decide to exit. For example, if you know how difficult it can be to find a suitable investment property, negotiate the price and arrange settlement, you will be pleased to find out that establishing an account with a stockbroker is as easy as opening a bank account. Having opened your account, you can buy and sell shares by giving instructions to your stockbroker over the telephone. Alternatively, you can use an online broker. Share prices are listed daily in the major newspapers and may be accessed online. ASX operates from 10 am to 4 pm Eastern Standard Time, Monday to Friday (excluding national holidays).

The ASX trading calendar, market hours and trading phases can be found on the ASX website: www.asx.com.au.

Liquidity and other market conditions

Investments with high liquidity not only make investing easier but, by allowing you to exit your investments easily, provide you with greater access to your money should you need it.

Share prices are determined by the buyers and sellers through the power of supply and demand, and trading may take place instantaneously. There is usually a healthy number of buyers and sellers for shares in most of the major companies. These are known as liquid stocks. However, the Australian market is noted for having a 'long tail'. This means that liquidity is quite concentrated and can trail off considerably outside the top 200 companies (and sometimes for stocks, within the top 200). You can readily determine how liquid the market for the shares in a particular company are by monitoring how many shares are sold on a daily or weekly basis. Another test of liquidity is how wide the spread is between the bid (the highest price people are prepared to pay) and the offer (the lowest price people are prepared to sell at). When there are lots of buyers and sellers, both sides compete to get their trade done so buyers are prepared to pay more and sellers are prepared to accept less, resulting in a narrowing of the bid/offer spread.

Interest-bearing investments also have a degree of liquidity. Generally speaking, the least liquid asset class is property: investors in this asset class may need to wait for the opportunity to realise any capital gain.

Minimum investment

The minimum investment for a particular asset class is another important consideration, as the amount required may prove to be prohibitive for some investors. In the case of share investment, some stockbrokers will accept an initial investment of as little as $500, but bear in mind your transaction costs (principally brokerage) if intending to make repeated small investments (see the section on 'Costs' that follows). Cash investments and managed funds also have low entry levels. While direct property has a higher entry level (usually at least $150 000), you can gain exposure to property using much less capital if you invest through a property trust (there is more on property trusts later in this chapter).

Costs

Investments often involve transaction costs when you buy or sell, as well as ongoing costs of ownership, and these must be taken into account when comparing asset classes. Transaction costs for direct sharemarket investments include brokerage payable to your stockbroker plus GST. There is no stamp duty payable on share transactions and there are no ongoing costs for direct sharemarket investments.

For other investments, transaction costs may include government charges, real estate agent commissions, entry and exit fees for managed funds and bank charges. Ongoing costs may include building maintenance, rates and letting agent fees, fund management fees and account fees.

Time frame for performance

The time frame required for your investment to perform is also an important consideration—some investments are better for long-term goals and others are more suited to short-term goals. The key determinants are the time left until the particular investment reaches maturity (the point at which you will be able to sell it) and/or the time required for it to perform to the desired standards.

Generally, shares do not have a maturity date and can exist for as long as the company is in operation. This means you can invest by taking a long-term view on performance. On the other hand, you can also take a short-term view. Day-traders aim to have opened a position and closed it out within the day, hence the name.

Property is generally considered as more of a long-term investment.

Two further considerations when determining the time frame you are prepared to accept for your investment to perform are the time it takes to invest and market timing.

Time it takes to invest

While ease of investment has already been discussed, the time it takes to be able to invest is also an important consideration. It takes time to learn to invest effectively—that is, time to learn about your investment alternatives, time to make investment decisions and time to manage your investments thereafter. Many people feel it is easier to invest in areas such as the cash market or managed funds than in areas such as property and the sharemarket.

Depending on the amount of time you have and your level of interest, you can:

¤ make all your sharemarket investment decisions by yourself

¤ rely more on the advice of your stockbroker

¤ make an indirect investment through a reputable fund manager.

The same applies to property—you can either research and decide on specific properties directly, or invest indirectly via listed or unlisted property trusts.

Of course, investment decisions become easier as you gain experience and learn more about the factors affecting your investment.

Timing

The timing of your investment in a particular asset class is also something to consider. Timing is particularly important when deciding when to buy or sell an investment in markets that have poor liquidity (a relative lack of buyers and sellers), as this characteristic tends to produce large price swings. Timing is also important for investors pursuing short-term investment returns or wanting to lock in capital gains. However, as most share investors are in the market for the medium to long term, the issue is not so much one of market timing as it is of their willingness to let time pass.

Choice and ability to diversify

The companies listed on the ASX include a number of large overseas-based companies. More than two-thirds of the listed companies are industrial, which includes businesses such as banking and retail. The remainder are part of the resource sector, which includes mining and exploration. Many listed companies are household names — for example, BHP Billiton, Westpac, Woolworths, Telstra and the Commonwealth Bank.

As an alternative, managed funds are popular because they provide investors with a cost-effective way to spread (diversify) their investment throughout local and overseas sharemarkets, as well as over other asset types, such as property and cash.

Another possibility is the growing range of exchange-traded products, including exchange traded funds (ETFs), which can give you quick exposure to a range of diverse assets with relatively low management fees. We talk about these more in chapter 10.

As well as internal diversification, another factor to take into account is which asset classes enable you to spread your investments over different levels of debt. The movements of interest rates paid and charged by banks have an effect on us all. For instance, if your bank increases its interest rates, the repayments on your mortgage are also likely to increase. Like most individuals, companies listed on the sharemarket have debts that need to be serviced. These debts, like a mortgage, are susceptible to movements in interest rates charged by the lender.

Direct property investment may offer fewer opportunities for internal diversification and spread of debt levels due to the amount of capital needed for each investment.

Taxation

Taxation can influence returns on investments significantly so it is an important consideration. However, don't let it be the sole determinant when making your investment decisions.

Characteristics of the asset classes

This section looks at the characteristics of the different asset classes. After cash, fixed-interest investments and property, the potential benefits and drawbacks of share investment are discussed in greater depth.

Cash and interest-bearing investments

Cash

The features of cash include:

- it usually provides the highest liquidity with the lowest risk
- it has zero growth
- it generally has no tax efficiency.

Cash management trusts may provide a higher return than a traditional bank account, and they may be useful for 'parking' your money between investments.

Interest-bearing investments

The features of interest-bearing investments include:

- they provide a potential steady income stream
- they usually give a greater yield/interest than cash
- they offer either fixed or floating rates of interest
- they allow you to diversify your portfolio and may reduce your risk
- the liquidity provided varies depending on the type of security and the market it is in

⊠ both the payment stream and any capital gain is likely to be treated as income for tax purposes

⊠ changing interest rates and company status can change the value of the security.

The role of interest-bearing investments

Interest-bearing investments entitle the investor to a predetermined fixed or floating rate of return and repayment of a capital sum on a fixed date. These securities are sometimes described as income investments because generally they provide a steady income return.

Interest-bearing investments may be useful as a stabilising influence on an investment portfolio and may reduce overall risk. These products may also be used as temporary havens in which excess cash or new funds may be placed to earn interest while you wait for other investment opportunities to arise.

When investing in unsecured notes, debentures or mortgages, it is important to spread your investments (and therefore your risk) across a number of companies and different industries. There should also be a spread of maturities so that any changes in the interest rates do not impact too heavily on your overall return.

You can access interest-bearing securities through the ASX, including:

⊠ *Corporate bonds or unsecured notes*—which are issued by financial institutions and companies for periods of between three months and five years, and offer a higher rate of interest than other interest-rate products of the same maturity as they are unsecured.

⊠ *Floating rate notes*—which are issued by similar entities as unsecured notes and return an interest amount that is determined by market interest rates (usually the bank bill rate). These securities may be perpetual, meaning they do not have a specific maturity date and investors enter or exit the market by buying and selling on the ASX.

⊠ *Convertible notes*—which are securities that pay interest like a bond but are convertible into ordinary shares of a company at a prescribed price or ratio at specified times and/or at maturity.

⊠ *Hybrid securities* — which are securities that are similar to convertible notes, but which pay a franked or unfranked dividend instead of interest at a fixed or resettable rate. They are convertible into ordinary shares of a company at a prescribed price or ratio at specified times and/or at maturity. These are considered a 'complex product' by the Australian financial regulator ASIC so they should be reviewed closely before making any investment decision.

Exchange-traded Australian government bonds (AGBs)

It has often been commented that Australian investors have their portfolios heavily weighted towards shares and/or property. In contrast investors in developed countries tend to have considerably more exposure to fixed-interest investments.

Perhaps one of the reasons Australians have been underweight in fixed interest is that government bonds have, for many years, been out of the reach of retail investors due to the large minimum investment amount required when purchasing bonds and the relative inaccessibility of the market for these bonds. Instead, those wanting the security and return of government bonds would invest in a managed fund that in turn invested in government bonds. Retail investors can now get direct exposure to Australian government bonds by buying and selling exchange-traded AGBs through ASX. There are free online courses that can teach you how exchange-traded AGBs work. Go to www.asx.com.au and look for the 'Education' button.

Market interest rates and credit-worthiness are the primary influences on the value of a bond. When investors purchase a bond and interest rates fall, the capital value of that bond will increase. Conversely, if rates rise, existing bond prices will fall. There is an inverse relationship between yield and price.

Most bonds carry a set interest rate (the coupon rate), which is paid at regular intervals, usually every six months, until the bond reaches maturity (the date the face value of the bond is repaid). It is important to understand that coupon rates (interest rates) for fixed-rate bonds do not change after they are issued. Although the real value of money may change over time due to market interest rates and inflation, the actual income flow will not.

The amount originally invested in a bond (usually in multiples of $100) is called the 'face value'. However, you may purchase a bond for more or less than its face value. The price depends on how much investors are willing to pay to earn the interest income provided by the bond. In other words, the coupon rate is usually fixed, but the market price of the bond can move up and down.

For example, say you purchase a $100 bond that pays 8 per cent interest semi-annually and is scheduled to mature in 10 years. Two years later, you decide to sell your bond. If by then interest rates on new bonds have fallen to 7 per cent, you will receive more than $100 when you sell your bond. Because an investor could now receive only 7 per cent from a new bond but your old bond still pays 8 per cent interest, your bond may now be worth more than $100. The gain in price of the bond has nothing to do with the quality of the bond—it is solely due to falling interest rates.

If, however, you decide to hold the bond for 10 years until maturity, you will receive your full $100 back and the interest that would be paid during the life of the bond.

The rule to remember is that bond prices move in an inverse manner to interest rates. If you bought a $10 000 face-value bond with an 8 per cent coupon for less than $10 000 (for example, $9000), your investment yield is higher than 8 per cent. If interest rates subsequently fall to 7 per cent, and the bond price increases, you could sell the bond for more than you paid for it.

A credit rating is given to most issued securities and also to the issuers of those securities. A downgrade or upgrade of these ratings will also either adversely or positively affect the capital value of these bonds.

Property

The features of property as an asset class include:

¤   it is a tangible asset

¤   it may not be easy to sell quickly

- it provides variable growth (and so has potential for loss or gain)

- over the long term, it may provide rental income returns

- there are several classifications to choose from, including residential, commercial, industrial and retail

- it may be a tax-effective investment, however you should consult your professional adviser on this matter.

As is the case with other classes of investment, there is the potential to lose in real estate. People can lose money in real estate for the following reasons:

- They buy in an area that is not growing in value. This may be due to a number of factors, such as slow employment growth, which reduces the demand for real estate from both tenants and buyers.

- They buy at inflated prices after a boom cycle.

- They overextend themselves by committing to loan payments that are too high for their circumstances.

- Their initial selection is poor. Remember the three golden rules when buying real estate — location, location and location.

Property can be held in a portfolio in several forms:

- home ownership for security

- direct property investment bought for capital gains and income

- indirect property investment through a listed or unlisted property trust.

Generally, direct investment involves the commitment of substantial amounts of capital, and is an illiquid investment. Also, a property can't be sold in parts — that is, you can't just sell the kitchen.

Unlisted property trusts

The features of unlisted property trusts include:

- the fund manager determines the portfolio

- there is usually a high cash component retained in case of redemptions — that is, the fund is not fully invested

- ¤ liquidity—that is, the manager's ability to repurchase—can vary depending on market conditions

- ¤ they have the ability to be a fund of funds—for example, a fund that invests in listed property trusts—which can be useful for smaller investors seeking greater diversification

- ¤ they may provide a relatively high yield with moderate growth.

Listed property trusts

Listed property trusts (LPTs) are also known as 'A-REITs'. LPTs are known globally as 'REITs': real estate investment trusts. In our case the 'A' differentiates the Australian market from overseas markets.

The features of listed property trusts include:

- ¤ there are specific classes available, including retail, commercial, industrial and CBD

- ¤ you can readily assess the liquidity of their market as they are traded on the ASX

- ¤ they may provide a relatively high yield and may provide tax efficiency and moderate growth

- ¤ they can represent good value when trading at a discount to net tangible assets

- ¤ they are usually less volatile than other types of shares as they are held by investors mainly for income purposes.

Shares and other sharemarket investments

Like other forms of investment, there are benefits and drawbacks associated with investing in shares. Below we set out a general description of the characteristics of shares, and in chapter 4 we will consider some of the risks involved in investing in shares.

The potential benefits provided by shares and other sharemarket investments include:

- ¤ they may provide good opportunity for capital growth and protection against inflation

- over the long term, they may provide a high overall rate of return
- some shares perform very well over the short term; however, some do not (three years is usually considered short term for investing in shares, with five to seven years considered medium term and longer than seven years considered long term)
- they may be an easy way to make a liquid investment if your choice includes some of the top 300 stocks
- direct share investment incurs entry and exit brokerage but no ongoing costs
- franked dividends may provide a steady, tax-effective income
- they may provide an effective means of diversifying your assets
- they may offer a high level of liquidity, allowing for ready access to your money
- sharemarket conditions are open and fair, with the security of your investment enhanced by regulation and active surveillance by the authorities.

The potential drawbacks of investing in shares include:

- unfranked dividends are subject to income tax at your marginal tax rate
- capital gains from share investments are subject to capital gains tax
- in the worst-case scenario, you can lose your total investment if you pick the wrong shares, as it is possible for shares to become worthless.

There is more detail on the risks and benefits of shares in chapter 4.

Overseas markets

With greater awareness of overseas markets and the increasing globalisation of our own marketplace, a growing number of Australian investors want to diversify their portfolio by investing overseas. Exposure to overseas markets allows Australian investors to add well-known global companies that are only listed on overseas exchanges to their portfolio.

Investing overseas allows you to diversify your investment portfolio with securities from markets and industry sectors that may experience higher growth rates than those in Australia. This is particularly important when you consider that Australia represents only about two per cent of the world's investment opportunities. The other 98 per cent is overseas. Investing in international securities also allows you to gain exposure in industry sectors that may not be as well represented in Australia, such as car manufacturing, pharmaceuticals and information technology. Being able to spread your risk and limit the impact of an adverse performance in any one economy, industry sector or currency is another advantage.

Of course, in making a decision to invest in international securities, you have to balance these advantages against the risks. While you take risks when investing in any security, trading in international securities has a number of additional risks, such as currency fluctuations, and you should only invest in international securities if you understand what they are and how they could affect your investment.

The risks involved with investing overseas may include:

¤ currency fluctuations

¤ changes in liquidity

¤ high volatility

¤ general market risks

¤ greater difficulty in finding sharemarket information

¤ commissions, taxes and other costs.

Before you decide to trade, you should carefully assess your experience, investment objectives, financial situation and tax status, and discuss your particular circumstances with your broker or financial adviser.

You can monitor the prices of international securities and the activities of companies from a number of sources. Historical and current information about companies can often be found on the company's website or the sites of overseas stock exchanges; or from cable television stations, your broker or various newspapers.

The importance of diversification

Most financial advisers recommend investing in a number of areas or asset classes to offset the risk of incurring a substantial loss or receiving an insufficient return in any one area. As different classes perform differently at different times, if you suffer a loss or a low return in one investment, this may be offset by stable or good returns in another investment. By diversifying your investments across a number of areas, you may reduce the risk of losing your hard-earned money.

While one area of investment may not suit your financial goals and objectives at a particular time, most financial advisers will recommend some form of investment in the sharemarket in order to create a balanced portfolio. Indeed, the discussion throughout this chapter has highlighted the many advantages of share investment.

The proportion of funds you allocate to sharemarket investment and how you go about making that investment will depend on your financial goals and objectives.

Diversification can refer to having a spread of investments across asset classes such as shares, property and fixed interest and there is also diversification within asset classes. For example, having a share portfolio comprising solely of bank shares would not be regarded as diversifying your risk. To effectively diversify, you need to take account of the correlation in performance between the shares of the companies you are considering buying.

As an example, see figures 3.1 and 3.2 (overleaf). Figure 3.1 charts the performance of the two big miners BHP Billiton and Rio Tinto. Although there are variations in performance, the tracking is close. Compare this to figure 3.2. This chart shows that the materials sector (mining, essentially) and the health-care sector diverge considerably.

Figure 3.1: ASX BHP and Rio Tinto daily prices over six months

Figure 3.2: ASX materials and health-care sectors daily prices over six months

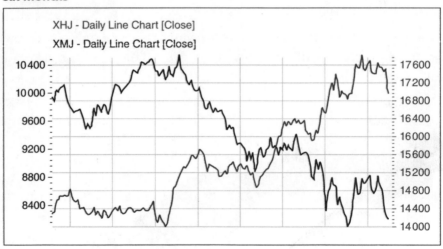

Inflation

While considering the benefits of different asset classes and how they fit in with your financial situation and investment objectives, a factor to consider across all asset classes is the effect of inflation on your investment. Inflation, even very low inflation, works against you by reducing the purchasing power of your money. For example, an annual inflation rate of just 2 per cent will reduce the real value of $10 000 to $7430 over 15 years. Table 3.1 shows the real value of $10 000 after 5, 10, 15 and 20 years at various rates of inflation.

Interest paid on a bank savings account may not be enough to keep you in front of inflation, especially after tax is paid on the interest income. Even when the inflation rate is low, interest rates are often low too, so your savings will continue to lose value.

Table 3.1: value of $10 000 after 5, 10, 15 and 20 years at various rates of inflation

Annual inflation rate	2%	4%	6%
Value at end of year 5	$9057	$8219	$7473
Value at end of year 10	$8203	$6756	$5584
Value at end of year 15	$7430	$5553	$4173
Value at end of year 20	$6730	$4564	$3118

To maintain the real value of your investment, your after-tax return must be higher than the inflation rate. For example, if inflation is running at 2 per cent per annum and your marginal tax rate is 30 per cent, you need to earn approximately 2.7 per cent interest on your bank account. A lower interest rate would result in the value of your savings eroding over time.

In the context of inflation and tax, return rates become even more important. The rates of return potentially provided by shares may exceed those offered by bank accounts and, therefore, may be a more effective hedge against inflation.

* * *

We have addressed the main asset classes and the different types of investment you can buy and sell through ASX. So now it's time to talk about the risks as well as the appeal of share investing.

CHAPTER 4

The benefits and risks of shares

All investments have pros and cons and since this book is principally about investing in the sharemarket, this chapter focuses on why people are attracted to shares and what they need to look out for.

Benefits

Let's have a look at some of the benefits of share ownership.

Capital growth — making a profit

People invest in shares because they offer the potential of generating good returns if share prices rise. Investors may only intend holding the shares for a relatively short time or they may have a longer term view, but in either case they hope to make a profit.

There is a saying that you have never made a profit until you have sold, which is quite true. You might buy some shares and be in the happy position of watching their price go up, and be reluctant to sell in case they keep on going up. You might then be in the less fortunate position of watching the share price go back down again. Your paper profit was just that—on paper, because you never sold. If you do sell at a profit you may be liable for capital gains tax.

Income

Apart from buying and selling shares for profit, investors also buy shares to provide an income stream in the form of dividends.

Dividends are cash distributions from a company to its shareholders. Dividend payments are typically paid each six months as 'interim' and 'final' dividends. Companies are under no obligation to pay dividends and the amount a company pays in dividends can vary from year to year.

Australian companies tend to pay higher dividends than elsewhere and high yield stocks are especially attractive for superannuants hoping to live on investment income.

Franking

Franked dividends are dividends that have been paid out of company income which has already been taxed in Australia. These can be fully or partly franked. A fully franked dividend is one paid from profits upon which the company has paid tax at the full company tax rate. At the time of writing, the rate of company tax is 30 per cent.

It is important to be aware that not all companies will pay dividends to shareholders. The decision to pay dividends usually lies with the board of directors—and dividends are generally only paid if the company has made a profit and paid tax on its earnings. As mentioned, the company may decide to retain profits to fund its growth. This means that dividends are not a certainty. They also may not be of a set amount or paid regularly.

Some people who invest for income do so in order to supplement their income from other sources and to support their lifestyle. Dividend income is subject to income tax at your marginal tax rate in each year it is received.

Imputation credits

Imputation credits are the tax credits that are passed on to investors via franked dividends and represent the tax already paid by the company.

Dividend imputation

Investing in shares may be tax effective; however, this is a topic on which you should seek specific and independent advice from a qualified adviser.

Prior to the introduction of dividend imputation, company profits paid out as dividends were effectively taxed twice—first at the company level and then at the shareholder level when the dividends were received.

As a result of dividend imputation, investors may benefit from the fact that tax has already been paid on the income received by the company they have invested in. In some cases, this enables investors to effectively receive their dividends tax-free. However, this is not always the case. The value of imputation credits (the credits attached to dividends on which tax has already been paid) is directly proportional to the rate of tax the company has paid.

This means that, under the tax system at the time of writing, if your marginal tax rate is less than 30 per cent you will not be required to pay any tax on the fully franked dividends you receive. In addition, the unused imputation credits may be used to offset tax payable on your other income or, in the event that there is no further tax payable, are refundable to you.

If your marginal tax rate is higher than 30 per cent, you will be required to pay some tax on fully franked dividends. However, the tax payable will be reduced by the value of the imputation credits attached.

Here are a couple of simple examples. Suppose a dividend is paid and suppose the company pays 30 per cent company tax and the dividend is fully franked.

Scenario 1

The shares are held by a superannuation fund that pays tax of 15 per cent. The tax paid by the company exceeds the tax that would be payable in the hands of the shareholder so the superannuation fund would receive a tax credit of 15 per cent of the value of the dividend.

Scenario 2

The shares are held by an individual on the top personal tax rate of 49 per cent. In this case the shareholder should have paid a higher amount of tax so the shareholder will have to pay 19 per cent tax on the dividend (49 per cent less 30 per cent).

Dividend reinvestment plans

Dividend reinvestment plans (DRPs—also known as dividend reinvestment schemes) enable shareholders to receive their dividends in the form of additional shares without paying brokerage for the transaction. From the company's point of view, this is a cost-effective way to raise additional funds from satisfied shareholders.

Dividend reinvestment schemes can be an effective way to grow your share portfolio. (You should consult your taxation adviser regarding the capital gains tax implications of purchasing shares through dividend reinvestment schemes, and careful record keeping is required.)

Company benefits to shareholders

In addition to sharing in a company's success via rising share prices and the receipt of dividends, owning shares in a company means you receive regular performance reports and you can participate in company meetings and be offered special share issues.

Shares in different companies (and different types of shares within the same company) may carry different rights and entitlements and it is important to understand the rights attached to the shares that you intend to purchase. We recommend that you discuss this with your broker or financial adviser prior to making any financial decisions.

Annual reports and company meetings

As a shareholder in a company, you will be keen to know how well that company is performing and what its plans are for the future. Public companies are required by law to report this information to their shareholders each year in the form of an annual report.

The annual report is your guide to the company's performance. The most important part of the annual report is its financial report.

The main components of a financial report

A financial report comprises:

- a balance sheet (showing assets and liabilities)

- an income statement (showing revenue and expenses)

- a statement of changes in equity (showing either all changes in equity, or changes in equity other than those arising from transactions with equity holders acting in their capacity as equity holders)

- a cash flow statement

- notes, comprising a summary of significant accounting policies and other explanatory notes.

Financial reports help you to find out what a company has earned during the year and the way those earnings have been distributed—that is, as tax paid to the government, dividends paid to shareholders or earnings retained to help fund the growth of the business. You can also find out how much debt the company has and where the main sources of cash are for the company. If you like reading the fine print, the 'Notes' are worth reviewing as many useful facts about the company's activities can be found there.

The annual report or its attachments will also contain a notice of the company's annual general meeting (AGM) and the business resolutions to be discussed there. After reading the annual report, you may decide to attend the AGM. Alternatively, you may decide to lodge the proxy form provided with the report to register your vote on any of the business to be discussed. Some companies are now providing the ability for their shareholders to vote electronically via their smartphones and to listen to or watch the AGM via the internet.

Whether or not you care to vote, attending the AGM will provide you with the opportunity to hear the chairperson and managing director speak on the company's activities and outlook for the year ahead. You will also have the opportunity to put forward any questions you may have on the business at hand.

Risks

Investors should be aware of the risk/reward relationship that exists with any type of investment. In order to receive a return on money invested you need to be prepared to place that money 'at risk'. Generally, the greater the risk associated with an investment the greater the rate of return investors should expect.

The risk of capital loss

An investment in the sharemarket is by no means a guaranteed investment.

In order to redeem the value of your shareholding you need to sell those shares on-market. If you own shares in a company that is performing poorly, it is possible that buyers may not be prepared to pay the price for which you want to sell your shares. As a result, you may be forced to sell your shares at a price much lower than what you bought them for.

What happens if you own shares in a company that goes out of business?

In the event that the company you own shares in goes out of business, its shares will no longer be tradable on the sharemarket. When a company is removed from the list of companies on the ASX, that company is said to have been 'delisted'.

If a company you own shares in has been delisted the only way to claim back your money is if a liquidator has been appointed and shareholders receive a portion of the sale of the company's assets.

In the event of asset liquidation, shareholders are last in the list of creditors (such as banks, other lenders and suppliers) to receive any funds that may be realised. As a result, shareholders may receive only a fraction of their original investment amount or could face the prospect of the complete loss of the amount they invested in the shares of that company.

Volatility risk

Share prices can rise and fall rapidly and investors must accept the fact that the value of their shares may fluctuate. General market risk may relate to a particular sector—for example, the resources sector may display more volatility than industrial companies. Think of the volatility of an oil exploration company in comparison to the shares of a major bank. Specific risk can relate to the performance of an individual company.

Timing risk

Because of market cycles, some companies have a higher degree of risk when the sharemarket has risen sharply and is set for a reaction. The opposite may apply when the market has gone into a strong decline and then starts to recover after showing some signs of stabilising. Not all sectors of the market follow the same price cycles.

Understanding business cycles and how different companies perform during the different phases of the business cycle may help you to manage the effects of timing risk.

The risk of poor-quality advice

Are the investment recommendations made to you supported by a thoroughly argued case or are they merely hearsay? The more reliable the information you have is, the better your decisions will be. Adopting a disciplined decision-making process may help you to minimise losses while you patiently build a portfolio. Recommendations involving high rates of investment return may fail to produce satisfactory results when taxation, ongoing fees and constant changes in investment cycles affect the performance.

Legislative risk

Your investment strategies or even individual investments could be affected by changes to the current laws. Are the companies within which you are considering buying shares in businesses that are subject to a high level of regulation? What is the likelihood of there being a change in regulations that may have an effect on the outlook for these companies?

Currency risk

If you have overseas investments, adverse moves in currency need to be considered. Your ability to convert overseas profits into Australian dollars will be affected by the prevailing exchange rate.

Individual or personal risk

This refers to the likelihood of changes occurring in personal circumstances (loss of job, illness or injury, or domestic changes such as marriage, divorce or a new addition to the family).

* * *

These are just some of the risks that are associated with an investment in the sharemarket. Learning about risk and its effect on your investments is crucial. You should clearly understand the risks associated with any investment you are considering.

In addition to your investment decisions, you need to know how to implement them; in the case of share investing this means buying and selling. Chapter 5 explains the different types of broker, getting ready to talk to one, placing orders and the paperwork you can expect when you buy and sell.

How to buy and sell shares

Before you can buy your first share on the sharemarket you need to find a stockbroker to act on your behalf. Only authorised market participants can buy and sell shares on the ASX.

Stockbrokers

There is a range of stockbroking firms and some have offices in regional centres as well as capital cities. Furthermore, online trading means there are many brokers offering services over the internet.

When advising clients, stockbrokers are legally obligated to take into account the financial situation and investment objectives of their individual client investors. A good adviser is one who understands your needs and speaks your language.

A stockbroker acts as your agent

Only stockbroking firms or their authorised representatives are able to buy and sell shares on the sharemarket. While other investment advisers may offer to buy and sell shares, ultimately these transactions can only be effected through an authorised market participant.

Stockbrokers and the client advisers employed as their representatives act as your agent in the sharemarket, providing advice and buying and selling securities on your behalf. While their advice may be provided free of charge, brokerage fees are charged for any buying or selling transactions.

All stockbroking firms must have a dealer's licence, which allows them to deal in securities. The authorised representatives (client advisers) they employ must be well qualified and up to date in their knowledge of sharemarket products and services. As mentioned, an important part of the role of client advisers involves knowing the financial situation and investment objectives of their clients.

A stockbroker to suit your needs

Not all stockbroking firms are the same. Choosing the best one for you will depend on the investment advice and additional services you need. While a few stockbroking firms concentrate largely on institutional business and focus on major fund managers, other stockbroking firms cater to private investors and have specific services and teams of client advisers dedicated to meeting their needs. You should make your selection on the basis of location, cost and, most importantly, the services and expertise provided.

Keeping these factors in mind, there are also other considerations when choosing a stockbroker, such as:

- Do you want a large or a small firm?
- Is your main concern the cost of brokerage?
- Do you want to trade online?
- Do you want advice and guidance?

Large versus small stockbroking firms

Many of the services provided by stockbroking firms require substantial resources, including a large number of staff. This is especially true of firms that conduct their research in-house, a process that requires a number of industry analysts to prepare reports and forecasts on individual companies.

Nonetheless, you may find that smaller stockbroking firms offer a more personalised service, focusing on your individual requirements while still providing access to professional research material, underwritings and other areas of investment.

Discount and internet stockbroking firms

Discount and internet stockbroking firms offer trading services only, meaning they will execute buy and sell orders on your behalf but they will not offer advice. Many of these firms charge a discounted rate of brokerage or a flat fee, depending on the size of the transaction. The rate may be discounted even further if orders are placed via the internet rather than by speaking to someone directly. Once they have an account with an online stockbroking firm, investors can access their online broker, place an order and monitor their portfolio, all with the click of a mouse. The service can be quick and easy to use once you have mastered the system. The benefits of trading online include easy access; low trading costs; and access to live share prices, research and market commentaries.

Some discount broking firms also offer research information, for which there may be a charge. Others have a pricing structure that includes monthly subscription fees, which allows investors to access the broker's research and market commentaries.

Obviously, one of the main advantages of using discount, non-advisory brokers is the low trading cost, but the disadvantage is that they don't give advice. A discount stockbroking firm may suit your needs if you prefer to make all your investment decisions yourself and have the time and resources to conduct your own research and analysis.

Full-service stockbroking firms

The main feature of full-service stockbroking firms is that they offer guidance and advice.

If you decide to use a full-service broker, you will be expected to answer a series of questions. This is because, when making recommendations, stockbrokers are obligated by law to 'know their client, know their product'. As a private client, you must therefore be prepared to provide your adviser with personal information.

You will be asked to provide information about your investment objectives: details of your need for income, capital growth, security, liquidity, your readiness to convert investments to cash and any proposed investment time frame. They will ask you about your income, your assets, your liabilities and your expenses. Importantly, they will want to know your appetite for risk.

Armed with this information, your adviser will be able to recommend the investment alternatives most appropriate to your specific needs and objectives. If this information is not provided, a stockbroker will only be able to provide a recommendation based on what is known of your situation.

Finding a broker

The Find A Broker service is available from the ASX website (www.asx.com .au). Alternatively, telephone ASX customer service on 131 279 to use the stockbroker referral service. You will be provided with the contact details for a number of stockbroking firms suited to your particular needs. It is advisable to contact each of them, outlining your needs and objectives, before deciding which firm or adviser you feel most comfortable with. After deciding on a firm, make an appointment to meet your adviser, as this individual may have a strong impact on your financial future.

Is my broker a 'participant'?

When looking to use the services of a stockbroking firm, you might like to check that it is a 'Participant of ASX'. These brokers come under the direct supervision of ASX and ASIC. They may also be participants of other licenced markets in Australia—for example, 'Participant of Chi-X Australia'.

There are other businesses that offer advice on buying and selling shares and they may offer a service to buy or sell your shares on your behalf. However, businesses that are not participants of a licensed market may not enter orders into the market. Instead they must go through a participant. You should establish the status of any party you deal with as certain compensation regimes are only available to clients of participants. Further information about the National Guarantee Fund can be obtained from Securities Exchanges Guarantee Corporation Limited at www.segc. com.au.

The process of buying and selling shares

You should always take your time before making investment decisions and placing orders with a stockbroker. However, once you have made up your mind, the actual process of buying and selling shares is easy because the stockbrokers do most of the work, regardless of their location.

Placing a buy or sell order is a straightforward process and trading takes place automatically (depending on liquidity for the share). Once the trade has taken place, you will receive a contract note (also called a confirmation) confirming any transactions and details for settlement. You will also receive a holding statement from each company's sub-register.

If you have registered through CHESS (we explain this system later in the chapter), whenever you buy or sell shares, CHESS maintains an electronic record of the transaction. A supplementary paper record, similar to a bank statement, will be mailed to you one month after the transaction has taken place. (There are no paper share certificates.)

Steps to buying and selling shares

There are two sides to every transaction. On one side are the buyer and the buyer's stockbroking firm; on the other, the seller and the seller's stockbroking firm. When you buy shares in companies listed on the ASX, you are buying them from investors who own them. You are not buying them from your stockbroker, or from the company itself.

Figure 5.1 (overleaf) summarises the standard procedure for a share transaction. The process is then expanded on over the following pages.

Figure 5.1: steps in a share transaction

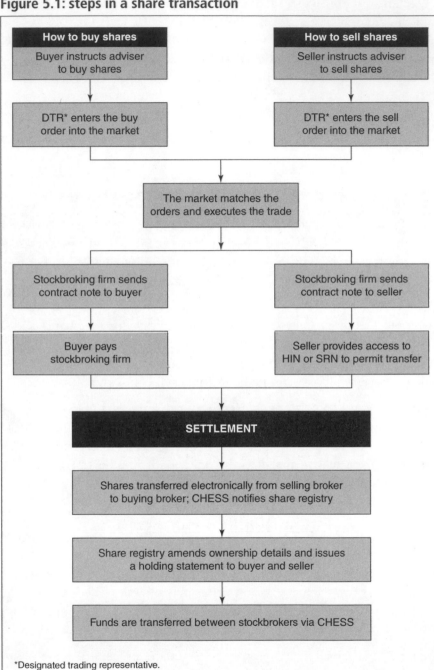

Unless you are interested in one of the more speculative companies (where large share price movements may occur quite suddenly) or you are considering buying shares in a float (in which case the application date becomes critical), there is usually no need to hurry your investment decisions.

Before placing your order, you should first check your financial situation and confirm that the proposed transaction suits your objectives. Then, when you are happy with your adviser's recommendation and/or your own research, you simply need to instruct your adviser to go ahead and buy or sell a particular number of shares on your behalf. Most stockbroking firms require you to forward the necessary funds before they will accept your first order to buy shares.

To start trading through an online broker, all you have to do is register with the broker and establish a cash management account or a direct debit or credit facility with a bank account. Once you have logged on, select the shares you want to purchase or sell using the ASX code, specify the number of shares, then enter the required buy or sell price before executing the trade.

With a full-service broker, once your relationship and account have been established you can place orders to buy and sell shares over the telephone. The stockbroking firm will invoice you later for the transaction.

When placing an order with your broker, it is a good idea to find out the current market price of the shares. Your adviser should also be able to tell you how many buyers and sellers are in the market for the shares and how they have traded over the day. You can also access this sort of information through most internet brokers. If placing orders over the phone, tell your broker the details of your order (company name and type of shares, number of shares and price at which you wish to buy or sell). Your broker should then repeat your order back to you.

The trading process

Once your order is placed, the trading process begins. Your stockbroker will enter your order into the market. The system will then compare buying and selling orders entered into the market and automatically execute trades in strict price–time priority whenever two orders match.

Every order is processed on an equal basis and larger investors do not get priority.

Your adviser will not necessarily call you when your order has been filled. However, if you place your order very near the market price of the shares, it may be filled while you are on the phone. Once you have placed an order and the transaction has taken place, you are required to fulfil your side of the transaction.

Your stockbroking firm will issue a contract note advising you of the details of the transaction. You may receive this soon after the transaction or it may be emailed to you at the end of the day. You should retain each contract note for your tax records, after first checking the following details:

¤   the company and type of shares

¤   the price at which the shares were traded

¤   brokerage.

The cost of your shares

You must pay for any shares you purchase within three business days after the transaction (this system is called T+3, meaning trade date plus three days; at the time of writing work was underway to go to T+2). Your costs will include the price of the shares and the brokerage payable to the stockbroking firm. Brokerage is also payable when you sell shares.

Brokerage

Brokerage fees differ between stockbroking firms. They are generally determined by the range of services offered, with higher fees often being charged to support research functions and other services.

Some firms charge a flat fee for transactions up to a certain limit, and most firms charge a minimum fee for all transactions. At the time of writing, minimum and flat fees range from approximately $20 (for online brokers) to $120 (for full-service brokers) per transaction.

You may be able to negotiate a particular scale of fees with your client adviser based on the volume of business you do. While some firms charge up to 2.5 per cent brokerage on smaller transactions, many firms charge between 1.5 and 2.0 per cent for the same service, with the percentage often reducing on transactions of higher value.

Completing your sharemarket transactions

As well as getting you set up with a trading account, your broker will also assist you in getting set up for settlement. You need to do this because when you buy or sell financial products such as shares, you must exchange the title or legal ownership of those financial products for money.

We will first explain the settlement process and then go through what you need to do.

Settlement occurs automatically three business days after a trade takes place. A system called CHESS (which is explained later in the chapter) automatically undertakes two simultaneous processes:

¤ payment is made for the trade by electronic transfer from the buyer to the seller

¤ the legal ownership of the share is transferred from the seller to the buyer.

This process is referred to as 'delivery versus payment' (DvP). The settlement process is handled by a settlement participant, who may be your broker or an agent contracted by your broker.

Which sub-register?

Any change of ownership needs to be recorded.

Your broker may ask you whether you want to be 'broker sponsored' or 'issuer sponsored'. If you choose the former, your shares will be held on the 'CHESS sub-register'. If you choose the latter, your shares will be held on a sub-register sponsored by the issuer of the shares that you have bought.

What's the difference?

If you opt for broker sponsored, all of your holdings can be consolidated on the one broker-sponsored account, making it easy to track your holdings and change any details—but you must trade through that broker while the shares are sponsored that way.

If you opt for issuer sponsored, you can easily trade through any broker but you will have a separate issuer-sponsored holding for each of the shareholdings.

You can have more than one broker sponsoring different shares within your overall portfolio. You can also switch shares from being broker sponsored to issuer sponsored, or vice versa, or from being sponsored by one broker to being sponsored by a different broker.

HINs and SRNs—the account numbers that identify your shareholdings

If you elect to go broker sponsored you will be provided with a HIN (Holder Identification Number) by your sponsoring broker. You will receive a different HIN for each broker.

If you elect to go issuer sponsored you will be provided with an SRN (Security-holder Reference Number) and you will have a separate SRN for each holding that you nominate as issuer sponsored.

In practice this can work as follows:

¤   You are broker sponsored and own shares in BHP, Telstra and NAB: you have one HIN.

¤   You own shares in BHP, Telstra and NAB and each of these is issuer sponsored: you have three different SRNs.

You can choose to have some holdings broker sponsored and other holdings issuer sponsored. In this case you would have one HIN and individual SRNs for the issuer-sponsored holdings.

It is important that you have your HIN and your SRNs recorded and handy as you will need these details when you contact your broker and company share registers.

Share registries

When you buy shares in a company, your ownership is recorded on that company's share register.

A company's share register is made up of all the shareholdings on its CHESS (broker-sponsored) and issuer-sponsored sub-registers combined.

The company's share registry looks after its share register and handles most of the dealings you will have with the company you have invested in.

You will be asked by the registry to provide banking details so that any payments such as dividends can be paid into your bank account. Company reports will be provided to you via the share registry as well as forms for voting on matters that require shareholder approval.

Many things can be managed online through the website of the share registry, although some matters may require written confirmation by the shareholder before they will be actioned by the registry (a change of address, for example).

Depending on how many companies you own shares in and the number of associated registries involved, you may have dealings with a number of share registries or just one or two.

Changing brokers

You may want to change stockbrokers at some stage. From a settlement administration perspective changing broking firms is straightforward. If your shares are issuer sponsored, you will need to complete a new client agreement form and provide some of your personal and financial details and the relevant SRN to your new broker.

If you have a HIN and you want to change your broker sponsor, this is possible; however, a fee may be applicable. Talk to your broker or ASX Customer Service for details.

CHESS statement explained

CHESS (Clearing House Electronic Sub-register System) is an electronic transfer and settlement system that has brought significant improvements to the Australian sharemarket. Securities of more than 2000 listed companies are held on CHESS.

Whenever you buy or sell shares involving a CHESS holding you will receive a CHESS holding statement, which confirms the transaction.

Likewise, whenever you buy or sell shares involving an issuer-sponsored holding you will receive an issuer-sponsored holding statement.

CHESS, on behalf of companies, issues holding statements to uncertificated shareholders who are sponsored by brokers or institutions that participate in CHESS. (A separate statement is issued for each security held in CHESS.) Figure 5.2 shows a sample CHESS holding statement. The main features of the statement are:

A   The company's name and logo.

B   Your name and address as registered in CHESS.

C   The security to which this statement relates.

D   The date the transaction is recorded in your CHESS holding.

E   The description of the transaction.

F   The transaction ID—this is a supplementary reference and may be useful for enquiries.

G   Information section—important messages will appear here.

H   The details of your CHESS sponsor—this is your first point of contact for any queries.

I   Your holder identification number—this is your unique CHESS number. Keep your HIN confidential and only disclose it in dealings with your CHESS sponsor.

J   Your balance in the security after being adjusted by the transaction.

K   The number of units that will increase or decrease your balance.

L   The ex/cum status—if the transaction was processed in the ex-dividend or cum-dividend period, it may appear here. (Note: 'cum' means 'with'; 'ex' means 'without'.)

Figure 5.2: a sample CHESS holding statement

(A)

Sample Company Limited
ABN: 12 345 678 910
Place of Incorporation: NSW

CHESS HOLDING STATEMENT

For statement enquires contact
your CHESS Sponsor:

PHILLIP CAPITAL LIMITED
LEVEL 12
15 WILLIAM STREET
MELBOURNE, VIC 3000

(H)

☎ **03 9876 5432**

(B)

SAMPLE COMPANY LIMITED
C/- MS JOAN ANN JONES
LVL. 12
123 BOUNDARY ST
SAMPLESVILLE QLD 1234

Holder ID Number (HIN):	1234567890
CHESS Sponsor's ID (PID):	05631
Statement Period:	February 2015
Page:	1 of 1

(I)

(C) — **SFI - ORDINARY FULLY PAID**

Date	Transaction Type	Transaction ID	Ex/Cum Status	Quantity On	Off	Holding Balance
17 Feb 15	Movement of Securities due to Purchase, Sale or Transfer	0179101225224900		500000		500000

(D) **(E)** **(F)** **(J)** **(K)** **(L)**

FOR YOUR INFORMATION

☞ To obtain full terms and conditions of an Issuer's securities contact the Issuer's Registrar or the Issuer directly.

☞ For information about CHESS Depository Interests (CDIs) and to obtain a free copy of the Financial Services Guide (FSG) or any supplementary FSG for CHESS Depositary Nominees Pty Ltd go to www. asx.com.au/cdis or phone 131 279.

☞ ASX Settlement may by law need to disclose information in CHESS Holdings to third parties.

☞ Do you have a small shareholding? Donate to Australian charities using ShareGift's brokerage-free service & receive tax deduction when over $2. www.sharegiftaustralia.org.au

Refer overleaf for additional important information

(G)

Share Registry Details:

ADVANCED SHARE REGISTRY
PO BOX 1156
NEDLANDS WA 6909
Ph: 08 9389 8033

ASX
SETTLEMENT CORPORATION

Issued By:
ASX Settlement Pty Limited | ABN 49 008 504 532 | PO Box H227, Australia Square, Sydney NSW 1215

As mentioned, a statement is issued whenever the holding balance of a security has been altered by a transaction during the month.

Ex/cum dividend

To be entitled to a dividend you must purchase a share before the ex-dividend date. Purchasing on or after the ex-dividend date means you will not be entitled to that dividend.

* * *

If you want to do your own buying and selling you will need to know what the market looks like on the screen of your online broker. Even if you decide to use an adviser to place your orders on your behalf you should still be able to understand and read the screen. So chapter 6 talks you through your first trade.

CHAPTER 6

Your first share trade

Once you have decided which shares to buy or sell and you are set up with your broker you are ready for your first trade.

What does the market look like?

When you are new to the sharemarket, one of the hardest things to understand is what the market actually looks like. Table 6.1 (overleaf) is an example of what you would typically see on a broker's website. It is the 'market depth' for a share — that is, the number of buy orders and sell orders that people have placed into the market.

Table 6.1: the market depth for a share

This column shows how many shares people are looking to buy at that price.	These two columns show you what people are willing to buy the shares for (the 'bid') and what they are willing to sell them for (the 'ask').		This column shows how many shares people are looking to sell at that price.
Quantity	Bid (the buyers)	Ask (the sellers)	Quantity
750	$1.21	$1.23	630
100	$1.20	$1.24	1000
5000	$1.20	$1.24	5000
500	$1.20	$1.24	600
20	$1.19	$1.25	5650

Price, volume and order type

In the example shown in table 6.1 you are looking to buy some shares. There are three basic points to consider:

¤ the price you are prepared to pay

¤ how many shares are available to buy at that price

¤ the type of order.

First, consider the price you are willing to pay. Using our example market in table 6.1, if you want to buy shares, the cheapest price they are available for in the market is $1.23—this is the price at the top of the 'Ask' column (see table 6.2).

Table 6.2: the cheapest price available for the share

| | | The lowest price being offered by sellers is $1.23. | |
Quantity	Bid (the buyers)	Ask (the sellers)	Quantity
750	$1.21	$1.23	630
100	$1.20	$1.24	1000
5000	$1.20	$1.24	5000
500	$1.20	$1.24	600
20	$1.19	$1.25	5650

Second, consider the number of shares you are looking to buy. In our example market there are 630 shares being offered for sale at the price of $1.23 each (see table 6.3).

Table 6.3: the number of shares you are looking to buy

| | | | There are 630 shares being offered for sale at $1.23 each. |
Quantity	Bid (the buyers)	Ask (the sellers)	Quantity
750	$1.21	$1.23	630
100	$1.20	$1.24	1000
5000	$1.20	$1.24	5000
500	$1.20	$1.24	600
20	$1.19	$1.25	5650

The third consideration is the type of order you use. Broadly speaking you can:

¤ set a particular price that you are happy to trade at—a 'limit' order, or

¤ ask for your order to be placed at the top of the price queue and traded at the best available price—a 'market' or 'market to limit' order.

Orders to buy and sell shares are typically matched first according to the best price and then according to the time at which they are entered into the system. This is known as price/time priority.

So, let's say you want to buy 500 shares and you are happy with a price of $1.23 per share. You place a market order. You can see from the market depth screen in table 6.4 that there is sufficient volume, so your order will trade. Tables 6.4 and 6.5 show what happens.

In table 6.4 you can see that your order for 500 shares has gone into the market and has traded with the other side.

Table 6.4: your order enters the market and trades

Quantity	Bid (the buyers)	Ask (the sellers)	Quantity
500	$1.23	$1.23	630
750	$1.21	$1.24	1000
100	$1.20	$1.24	5000
5000	$1.20	$1.24	600
500	$1.20	$1.25	5650
20	$1.19	$1.25	100

In table 6.5 you can see that your order for 500 shares has been executed and so it disappears from the list of orders and the next best buy order ($1.21) becomes the top order on the bid side. Your order for 500 shares did not fill all the shares on offer at that price, so there are still 130 left at $1.23 on the ask side.

Table 6.5: the market adjusts to show that your order has been executed

Quantity	Bid (the buyers)	Ask (the sellers)	Quantity
750	$1.21	$1.23	130
100	$1.20	$1.24	1000
5000	$1.20	$1.24	5000
500	$1.20	$1.24	600
20	$1.19	$1.25	5650
700	$1.18	$1.25	100

Let's extend this example and consider a scenario where you want to buy 4000 shares. You have two options:

¤ place a market order, in which case you will need to accept a combination of prices at $1.23 and $1.24 to fill the volume of your order

¤ place a limit order for a price you choose, say $1.22, and see if there are sellers in the market who will lower their price to meet your order and complete a trade.

It is important to note that the volume of buying and selling of shares in a company is known as liquidity. This is an important consideration because the more liquid a stock is, the easier it is to buy and sell quickly at the price you expect.

Many companies have very active markets for their shares, with millions of dollars' worth of shares traded every day. But there are also companies that have relatively little activity in their shares. The difference between the buy price and the sell price (the bid/ask spread) may be quite a bit wider for an illiquid stock than for a liquid stock. If you want to buy a larger quantity of shares of an illiquid stock, you may have to pay quite a bit more than the current sell price to get all of your order filled.

Our example does not convey the dynamic nature of the sharemarket. During trading hours, the price of a share can be constantly moving, sometimes by large amounts. Buying and selling shares does require attention and diligence as the price of a share can move very rapidly.

Using a limit order is one way to be sure of the price you expect to trade at. Let's look at limit and market orders more closely.

Limit order

A limit order enables you to be specific about the price you want to trade at.

This means that for a buy order the price you nominate is the maximum price the order will trade at. It can trade at less than this price, but not more. Using our example, you might place a limit order for $1.22 — this is less than the current best price being offered for sale. The market might move to meet your price, in which case you have bought the shares at a cheaper price than if you had simply bought the shares at $1.23 each.

A limit buy order at $1.22 can trade at $1.21, but it will never trade at $1.23 or higher.

For a sell order, the price you nominate is the minimum price the order will trade at. It can trade at more than this price, but not less. For example, a limit sell order entered at $1.23 can trade at $1.24, but it will never trade at less than $1.23.

Market or market to limit order

A market to limit order is commonly referred to as a market order. If you are happy to trade at the best prevailing price in the market, you can use this order. With this order type you nominate the quantity you wish to buy or sell, but not the price.

The principle of this order type is that you will trade at the best price available in the market. In the case of our example, you would buy shares at $1.23, the best price at which they are being offered for sale. If the whole volume of your order can't be traded at this price, the remainder of the volume is then converted to a limit order at the price you traded.

In practice, brokers may offer a modified version of this where your market order executes with some margin around the first traded price to ease the execution of the order. This increases the convenience of this order type, giving you more confidence that your order can be promptly executed and filled.

Different brokers have different arrangements regarding how they manage market/market to limit orders so make enquiries with your broker.

*   *   *

Some people get involved in investing because they are offered shares in a float. Other investors like to get in on floats before companies list as a buying opportunity. So in addition to buying and selling on-market it is important for you to know how floats work.

CHAPTER 7

Buying shares in a float

Chapter 6 explained the process of buying and selling shares already listed on the sharemarket. This is the activity that the majority of people are engaged in when they participate in the sharemarket.

However, before shares can be bought and sold on the sharemarket, they are issued in the primary market by companies via a float or initial public offering (IPO).

The same fundamental analysis principles and methods are required whether you are buying shares in a new float or buying existing shares. The major differences are that the principal source of information in a share float is the product disclosure statement, also known as a prospectus, and there is no share price or dividend history.

The product disclosure statement

Companies seeking to list on the ASX must offer new shares to the public by way of a product disclosure statement (PDS, commonly called a prospectus). The PDS is a very important document which, once prepared, must be lodged with ASIC. Among other things, a PDS is required by the *Corporations Act 2001* (Cth) to contain all the information that investors and their professional advisers would reasonably require to make an informed assessment, including:

¤ the rights and liabilities attached to the securities offered

¤ the assets and liabilities, financial position and performance, profits and losses, and prospects of the body that is to issue (or that issued) the shares, debentures or interests.

Five questions to ask

When looking at investing in a share float, it is important to be able to answer the following five questions:

¤ *Who* is involved? For example, stockbrokers, underwriters, management, board or others.

¤ *What* is on offer? For example, growth, income-yielding, tax-effective or speculative stocks.

¤ *When* does the issue take place? For example, during a bull or a bear market.

¤ *Why* are they raising funds? For example, for expansion, or to retire debt, sell down or attempt a takeover.

¤ *How* can you participate in the issue? For example, through public pool, firm share or entitlement.

This process may seem a little simplistic, but by trying to answer each of these questions you should be able to focus better on the issues at hand. You can obtain a particular PDS from the underwriter of the issue or the sponsoring stockbroking firms. Who is involved, why they are raising funds and how you can participate in the issue are discussed below, as well as how to analyse your investment opportunity.

Who is involved?

The PDS should contain an outline of the managers and directors of the company. As well as giving some background information on these people, it should disclose any financial interests they may have in the company.

Often, shares will be issued to the existing owners (and even to the underwriters) as payment for existing assets. These are called 'vendor' shares. A prospective investor needs to determine whether these vendor shares appear a fair and reasonable payment for the assets of the company.

You should also see if there are any constraints on the sale of vendor shares. This is referred to as 'escrow'. Shareholders should be aware of that period and watch for any possible sales of vendor shares as this is often a danger period for the share price.

Is the float underwritten?

A general definition of an underwriter is a person or organisation that agrees to bear a risk or a portion of risk (sub-underwriter) in return for a fee or premium. If the public and institutions do not take up all the available shares on offer, the underwriter is obligated to take up what is left. This means the company issuing the capital is assured of raising the money. The underwriters are usually stockbrokers or merchant bankers. They are paid a fee for guaranteeing the issue.

The fee charged by the underwriter should be disclosed within the PDS. Markets generally take a negative view of an underwriter who is left with shares, as the unplaced parcel then 'overhangs' the normal course of daily trading. Underwriters are not long-term holders of shares and therefore generally attempt to place the shares as soon as possible.

Company profile

A well-prepared PDS provides potential investors with a well laid out schedule of a company's history and financial situation and a general overview of its operations. This information is most useful in situations where investors are not already fully aware of the nature of a company's business operations.

In some situations, a PDS relates to a new venture or activity and it is therefore unable to offer the same degree of historical information.

Board of directors

When reviewing the list of board members, ask yourself:

¤ Is their experience relevant to the company's activities?

¤ Have they been associated with other companies? Are these companies successful?

¤ Have they been or are they associated with any unsuccessful or failed operations?

Also consider the credibility of their information. Do they provide you with any non-financial details to help you make your decision? Do they have 'vision'? (In any business, vision is very important.)

Why is the company raising funds?

Sharemarket activity is driven by the basic need for capital (money). Whether it is to be used to fund a new invention, to facilitate a merger or acquisition or to reduce liabilities, it all boils down to one thing—ready access to cash. You should be comfortable with a company's reasons for seeking new capital before you buy shares in it.

Pricing

An underwriter/corporate adviser may price the issue at a discount to the perceived value in the market to help ensure that the issue is fully subscribed. Such pricing may allow for some gains to be made on listing (called stag profits), and create a liquid secondary market. There may also be added attractions to entice investors, such as early availability of dividends, franking credits or simply the promise of high yields.

Frequently asked questions

Here are some of the questions investors ask about floats.

What happens if my application is rejected?

Should your application be rejected or your allocation be reduced, your money will be refunded to you.

What costs are associated with buying shares through a float?

There are no costs other than the purchase price of the shares. Brokerage is only charged on trades performed on the secondary market — that is, after the shares are listed.

When will the shares begin trading?

An approximate date the shares list on the sharemarket and begin trading will be stated in the PDS; however, this date may be subject to change. Your stockbroker or client adviser will be able to advise you of the precise listing date closer to the actual event, as will the financial media (particularly for large public floats).

Where do I lodge my application?

You can send your application and cheque to the address stated on the application form within the PDS. Alternatively, if consulting a client adviser or stockbroker the application may be lodged at the stockbroking office, or via the broker's website.

My current broker has offered me 'firm stock'. What does this mean?

In many cases, stockbrokers are able to secure a quantity of shares in a float, some of which they can guarantee will be allocated to you. However, this may only apply to specific clients.

What is a 'deferred delivery settlement'?

Many floats will list on the secondary market before the company's share registry has been able to issue statements and holder identification numbers (HINs). If a float trades 'deferred delivery', you will not receive settlement (payment) for shares you sell until the deferred date.

For example, say XYZ Ltd lists on 4 May on a deferred settlement basis for 11 May. If you sell your shares immediately after the shares list on 4 May, you will not be paid until 11 May, which is the first settlement date for the share.

Finding out about new floats

The ASX website (www.asx.com.au) lists all the upcoming floats for companies that have lodged documents with the exchange. You can find this information from the 'Prices and Announcements' tab on the home page of the ASX website. However, bear in mind that you may read about an upcoming float that is not listed on the ASX site. This is because ASX only lists those floats where documents have been lodged, whereas media reports may report on floats that are not yet at this stage. For this reason it can be useful to also monitor the financial media and broker websites, as well as subscribing to newsletters.

* * *

There is more to the market than deciding what to buy and sell and placing your order. There are different types of securities, they all have their own coding convention and there are other codes that can be displayed on screen which mean different things. And then there is the matter of what happens in the various market phases. It is being across the detail of these nuts and bolts that will round out your understanding of the market.

CHAPTER 8

The nuts and bolts of the sharemarket

In addition to decisions about which asset classes—and which assets within these asset classes—you are going to invest in, you also need to navigate the actual buying and selling of these assets. When it comes to shares, that usually means the sharemarket. In this chapter we will take you through the various types of securities and company codes, what the markets for stocks actually look like on the screen and what you can do if you want to transfer shares off-market.

Types of securities

Shares may be one of the simplest financial products in which to invest, but there are different types of shares traded on the ASX, each with different characteristics.

It is important to understand these distinctions because the characteristics of different types of shares can significantly affect the way you decide to invest. The different types of shares include:

¤   ordinary shares

¤   preference shares

¤   trust units

¤   stapled securities

¤   partly-paid shares.

Ordinary shares

Most shares traded on the ASX are 'ordinary' shares. Ordinary shares carry no special or preferred rights. Holders of ordinary shares usually have the right to vote at a general meeting of the company, and to participate in any dividends or any distribution of assets on winding up of the company on the same basis as other ordinary shareholders.

Preference shares

Preference shares usually give their holder a priority or 'preference' over ordinary shareholders to payments of dividends or on winding up of the company. There are different kinds of preference shares with different rights and characteristics. Holders of preference shares usually have voting rights that are restricted to particular circumstances or particular resolutions; however, this will depend on the terms of the shares.

Trust units

Trust units are increasingly popular in the form of property trusts, equity trusts and cash management trusts. While unitholders have less control than shareholders, from an investor's point of view units in listed trusts are similar to ordinary shares except that, instead of a dividend, a full distribution of profit is made to unitholders.

Stapled securities

A stapled security is where investors own two or more securities that are generally related and bound together through one vehicle. Typically, stapled securities consist of one trust unit and one share in the funds management company that can't be traded separately.

The trust holds the portfolio of assets, while the related company carries out the funds management and/or development opportunities. Figure 8.1 shows a typical stapled security structure.

Figure 8.1: an example of a stapled security

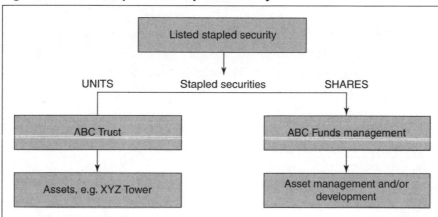

Partly-paid shares

Partly-paid shares (also known as contributing shares) are issued without the company requiring payment of the full issue price. These instruments can appeal for things such as infrastructure projects where not all the capital for the project is required at the outset. At a specified future date or dates, the company is entitled to call for all or part of the outstanding issue price, and the shareholder at the time the call is due is legally obliged to pay the call. (No-liability companies are not required to specify the date or dates on which calls will be made, and the shareholder at the time the call is due may pay the call or forfeit the share.)

Partly-paid shares traded on the ASX are usually identified by a five-letter code consisting of the company code and a two-letter suffix, generally CA to CZ (not including CP).

Generally, a holder of a partly-paid share has the same rights as an ordinary shareholder to vote, and to dividends on winding up of the company, but those rights will be proportional to the amount paid on the share (except for a vote by show of hands, where a holder of a partly-paid share has one vote, the same as any ordinary shareholder).

Retail investors are now required to sign a client agreement with their broker before first trading in partly-paid shares, to acknowledge that they understand the risks involved. This requirement was introduced after investors got caught out when they bought partly-paid shares and did not realise they were legally obligated to pay additional contributions when called upon to do so by the issuing company. In some cases the subsequent payments required were significantly higher than the initial outlay and some investors did not have the funds to meet their obligations. This is why much fuller disclosure of the obligations of partly-paid shares is now required.

Rights and bonus issues

Companies can make special issues of rights or bonus shares to shareholders. As a shareholder, it is important to understand what each issue entails and the dates involved. If you have any doubt about such issues, you should contact your adviser.

Bonus issues

Bonus issues are shares issued free of charge to shareholders. Bonus issues are made on a predetermined pro-rata basis—for example, 1-for-5. This means you will receive one new share for every five you own. For example, if a company in which you hold 1000 shares announces a 1-for-10 bonus issue, you are entitled to 100 extra shares at no cost, which would bring your total holding to 1100 shares. Once a bonus is issued, the share price usually drops as the value of the company's assets is now spread over a larger number of shares. Bonus shares dilute the market price of the shares in direct proportion to the increase in the total number of shares on issue.

This price adjustment occurs on the ex-bonus (XB) date. An investor who buys the existing shares on or after the XB date is not entitled to the bonus shares—they belong to the previous owner of the shares. The closing date is the date on which the company closes its books to determine which shareholders are registered to receive the bonus. Hence it is important for investors to remember the XB date if they are considering buying shares in a company that is offering a bonus issue.

Rights issues

A rights issue entitles existing shareholders to take up additional shares in the company at a below-market price without having to pay brokerage. Rights issues enable the company to raise additional funds from shareholders for expansion or to repay debt. The process for a rights issue is similar to a float insofar as a product disclosure statement is prepared and an underwriter is often appointed. Shares are offered on a predetermined pro-rata basis—for example, one for four. This means that for every four shares you own, you can purchase an additional share at the discounted price.

A rights issue may be renounceable or non-renounceable. Renounceable means shareholders are entitled to sell their rights to other investors on the sharemarket if they do not wish to take up the additional shares themselves. Non-renounceable means only existing shareholders can participate and they must either take up the shares or forfeit the rights. If you are not a shareholder and wish to be, you may be able to purchase renounceable rights from shareholders who did not want to take up the rights and preferred to sell them.

To take up shares in a rights issue the shareholders complete a form and submit a cheque for the number of shares they want. The form is lodged with the company's share registry, so the transaction is done off-market and does not incur brokerage. Shareholders are not obliged to take up their full allocation.

Companies usually structure the rights issue so that the cost of purchasing new shares is at a slight discount to the market price at the time of issue or alternatively at a discount to a price established at the close of the offer. This makes sense because otherwise shareholders may prefer to just buy the shares on market.

Let's look at an example.

Assume you own 10000 XYZ shares and a 1-for-5 renounceable rights issue is made. The shares are currently trading at $10 and the rights offer entitles you to take up additional shares at a price of $9 per share. As you own 10000 shares you are entitled to purchase up to 2000 additional shares.

If you wanted to buy the full allocation you would send in a cheque for $18000 ($9 × 2000). If you only wanted 500 shares you would send in a cheque for $4500. If you elected to not take up the offer at all or to apply for less than your full allocation you might consider selling your remaining rights on-market because in this example the rights are renounceable.

It follows that because the new shares are being issued for a price lower than the current market, this will have a diluting effect on the value of the existing shares. The bigger the discount to the current prices of the shares, the greater the dilution effect of the rights issue.

Market announcements

Companies are required to provide a steady stream of information to the market. This assists investors in making informed assessments about the suitability of a particular company's shares for their portfolio. The market announcements are important to the active investor. Announcements providing information about the prospects of a company and those describing growth strategies by senior company board members or the CEO are of particular use.

The ASX's continuous disclosure regime is based on the principle that information that may affect share prices or influence investment decisions must be disclosed. Investors can find all market announcements published live and freely available on the ASX website. In general, listed companies must lodge the following with the ASX:

¤ annual report

¤ half-yearly report

¤ preliminary final report

- half-yearly ASIC accounts

- annual audited financial statements lodged with ASIC

- quarterly cash flow report—only required for mining exploration entities and commitments test entities

- quarterly activities report—for mining exploration or production entities

- takeover information

- security holder notifications.

To find out when to expect the routine announcements, such as annual reports, you can refer to the Reporting Calendar available on the ASX website (www.asx.com.au).

Codes, codes and more codes

The massive amount of data communicated via feeds and displayed on screens means there is a need to abbreviate wherever possible. Securities, security types, indices and trading conditions all have codes.

What is a ticker code?

Anything traded on financial markets has an individual code that uniquely identifies it in an abbreviated form. You may be familiar with these codes, which are displayed on ASX ticker boards and are included alongside company names in newspaper sharemarket tables.

Codes uniquely identify a tradeable instrument so that it can be tracked throughout trading, settlement and price reporting systems. These codes are important. Whenever you make an order to buy or sell you will need to know the ASX code for the instrument you want to trade.

ASX sometimes uses a different length of ticker code to indicate to investors and traders that there is something different about a listed product.

A good rule to remember is that a three-character code typically indicates the ordinary shares in a company. Where there are more or fewer than three characters, there is most likely something different from the ordinary shares of a company.

ASX will have regard to certain principles when allocating codes to products that can be found on the ASX website.

How many characters are there in ticker codes?

Initially, all codes were confined to three characters; however, formats have grown considerably due to the number and types of instruments now available for trading. There are far more companies listed these days and there are other markets such as options, warrants and futures that also require codes.

Listed companies — the ASX three-character code

Most ASX listed companies' codes have three characters. This three-character code represents that company. All securities issued by that company will incorporate its three-character code.

The three-character code is typically used for the primary issue of shares by that company. This is the case for listed companies, A-REITs, listed investment companies, infrastructure funds and conventional exchange traded funds.

Listed companies — secondary issues

A company may issue options that can be exercised for shares traded on-market. For example, an option over XYZ Company may have the code XYZO and a rights issue may use the code XYZR.

The Telstra fully-paid ordinary stock code is TLS; however, at the time of its capital raising through an instalment receipt (IR) structure those instalment receipts traded as TLSCA, indicating that there were differences between Telstra ordinary shares and the instalment receipts.

Special-condition codes

A fourth character that is added to the underlying three-character codes indicates a special circumstance or product type. For example, if ASX undertook a share split, it may trade on a deferred settlement basis for a period. This would be identified by the code ASXDA.

For a partly-paid security where an additional payment of money is required to be made by the holder, the security would be identified by the fourth character, 'C'; for example, ASXCA.

Listed companies—bonds and hybrids

Listed companies may issue various types of interest-rate securities. These securities have a four-, five- or six-character code. Again, the three-character issuer code will be the prefix, followed by a character to identify the type of security (for example, H: unsecured note; G: convertible note; or P: preference share).

A company may issue a series of a particular type of interest-rate security. In this case it becomes necessary to be able to identify each particular series. Alpha characters are added sequentially to each series as they are issued. For example, WOWHA represents the first unsecured note on issue by Woolworths Limited and CBAPB represents the second preference share issue by the Commonwealth Bank of Australia.

Exchange-traded products (ETPs)

ETPs include exchange-traded funds (ETFs), managed funds and structured products. These products may have three-, four- or six-letter ticker codes.

Share price indices

Share price indices are identifiable by a three-character code. It is useful to remember that the code for the S&P/ASX 200 is XJO and that the prefix XJO is used for all exchange-traded options and warrants over the S&P/ASX 200 index.

Index codes are also used to plot the performance of various indices on a chart. The ASX website provides more information on the various coding conventions as well as a helpful tool for looking up the codes for various companies and financial instruments.

ASX trading hours and market phases

It is helpful to have an understanding of the trading hours and the key market phases because your order will be treated differently depending on when it was entered. For example, if you enter an order before the market opens it will become part of the opening phase, whereas this will not be the case if your order is entered when normal trading has commenced. (These phases are correct as at March 2015 and include bonds, hybrid securities, exchange-traded products and managed funds.)

The market goes through a number of phases on any trading day. The particular market phase determines the type of action that may be taken for an order on ASX Trade (the ASX trading system), which in turn affects how trading is conducted.

Pre-opening phase

Pre-opening takes place from 7 am to 10 am, Sydney time. During pre-opening:

⌑ brokers enter orders into ASX Trade in preparation for the market opening

⌑ investors may enter orders online. The orders are queued according to price–time priority and will not trade until the market opens.

Opening phase

Opening takes place at 10 am Sydney time and lasts for about ten minutes. ASX Trade calculates opening prices during this phase. Securities open in five groups, according to the starting letter of their ASX code:

⌑ *Group 1:* 10:00:00 am +/– 15 seconds 0–9 and A–B; for example, ANZ, BHP

⌑ *Group 2:* 10:02:15 am +/– 15 seconds C–F; for example, CPU, FXJ

⌑ *Group 3:* 10:04:30 am +/– 15 seconds G–M; for example, GPT

⌑ *Group 4:* 10:06:45 am +/– 15 seconds N–R; for example, QAN

⌑ *Group 5:* 10:09:00 am +/– 15 seconds S–Z; for example, TLS.

The time is randomly generated by ASX Trade and occurs up to 15 seconds on either side of the times given above; for example, group 1 may open at any time between 9:59:45 am and 10:00:15 am. So, if you are interested in a stock commencing with a ticker code that starts with the letter 'A' you can expect an opening price and initial trades to be completed quite soon after 10 am. The further down the alphabet the company's ticker code is, the longer it will take.

Normal trading

Normal trading takes place from 10 am to 4 pm, Sydney time. Brokers enter orders into ASX Trade and ASX Trade matches the orders against each other in price/time priority on a continuous basis. The vast majority of trades take place during normal trading.

Pre-CSPA

Between 4:00 pm and 4:10 pm, Sydney time, the market is placed in Pre-CSPA. Trading stops and brokers enter, change and cancel orders in preparation for the market closing.

Closing single price auction

The closing single price auction takes place between 4:10 pm and 4:12 pm, Sydney time.

ASX Trade calculates closing prices during this phase. This is important because a lot of calculations are based on closing prices.

Status notes

There are a number of codes used by the trading system to provide further information about the trading status of a security. These codes are known as status notes.

You may not have much interest in these condition codes now, but when you come to buy and sell you will see these codes on screens and you will need to understand what they mean. A complete list is displayed on the ASX website, together with an explanation for each, but here are some key ones.

XD—ex dividend

XD shown against a company's three-letter ASX code means the security is currently quoted on an ex-dividend basis and that trading in this security does not carry the entitlement to the dividend payment. If there is no code displayed alongside a security, then the security is trading on a cum basis where cum means 'with'. To be entitled to a dividend you must purchase the share before the ex-dividend date.

XB—ex bonus issue

XB displays for a security from the morning of the ex-bonus date and remains until the close of trading on the bonus issue date. Trading in a security displaying XB does not carry the right to receive the bonus issue. All orders are purged at the end of the trading day prior to the security being quoted on an XB basis.

XC—ex return of capital

XC first displays for a security from the morning of the ex-capital return date and remains until the close of trading on the payment date. Trading in securities displaying XC on the trading system does not carry the entitlement to the return of capital payment. All orders are purged at the end of the trading day prior to the security being quoted on an XC basis.

XI—ex interest

XI first displays for a security from the morning of the ex-interest date and remains until the close of business on the payment date. XI indicates that interest has been paid on the securities. Trading in securities displaying XI does not carry the entitlement to the current interest payment. All orders are purged at the end of the trading day prior to the security being quoted on an XI basis.

XR—ex rights issue

XR first displays for a security from the morning of the ex-rights date and remains until the close of business on the application's close date. Trading in securities displaying XR does not entitle the holder to receive securities in the rights issue. All orders are purged at the end of the trading day prior to the security being quoted on an XR basis.

Off-market transfers

You do not have to buy or sell your shares on market, although it is by far the most common way. A typical situation where you may not want to transfer via an on-market transaction would be a transfer between family members or transfers from deceased estates. Off-market transfers do not use a stockbroker as the intermediary; instead, the transfer is executed through the use of an Australian standard transfer form. Off-market transfers of securities held on the CHESS sub-register occur electronically through CHESS. The Australian standard transfer form is not required for transfers through CHESS. For this type of transfer you will need to go through your stockbroker.

To obtain an Australian standard transfer form, contact the share registry of the company whose shares you wish to transfer, or go to the Securities Registrars Association of Australia Incorporated website, www.sraa.com. au. For advice on completing the form, consult your stockbroker or financial planner.

Reading share price tables—common terms

In addition to business news about listed companies, many websites and newspapers publish tables of information on share prices, changes in value and volume of trades from the previous ASX trading day. See table 8.1 (overleaf), for example.

Table 8.1: sample per share price

Company name	Last sale price	+ or −	Quote		52 week		Dividend		
			Bid	Offer	High	Low	Rate	Yield %	PE ratio
AMP Ltd	5.42	+7	5.41	4.420	5.96	4.11	13.00p	4.37	24.19
Ansell Ltd	22.37	+2	22.37	22.39	23.00	17.73	42.00	1.87	71.86
Argo Invest.	7.89	−1	7.86	7.89	8.14	7.18	28.00f	3.55	26.09
ASX Ltd	36.67	−1	36.66	36.67	37.93	34.07	178.08f	4.86	18.47
BHP Billiton Ltd	27.36	−61	27.36	27.37	39.79	27.29	131.00f	4.68	10.13
Coca-Cola Amatil	9.14	+16	9.13	9.15	12.35	8.19	52.00f	5.59	23.1

Let's have a look at some of the information in the table:

¤ *Bid*—the price at which someone is prepared to buy shares.

¤ *Offer*—the price at which someone is prepared to sell shares.

¤ *Price range for 52 weeks*—the range of prices over the last 52 weeks.

¤ *Dividend rate*—the dividend shown as cents per share. This figure may be followed by 'f', which means fully franked, or 'p', which means it has been partly franked.

¤ *Dividend yield*—the dividend shown as a percentage of the last sale price for the shares.

¤ *P/E ratio*—the number of times the price covers the earnings per share.

A great deal of information is available via the internet. This includes the ASX's website, brokers' websites and listed companies' websites. Some of the most popular information from these sources is company reports, daily company announcements, historical and current share prices, and company news.

*   *   *

For many people, the strongest association with the sharemarket is when they hear about movement in the share price index in the evening news. Indices can be a great barometer of how the market is faring, but you need to know what they are measuring and how they measure it.

CHAPTER 9

Following the
S&P/ASX indices

References to sharemarket activity can be heard on the television news every night. This information can provide a simple and easy way of following the market if you understand the meaning of the information provided. For example, a typical sharemarket report may sound like this:

> After a slow start, turnover on the sharemarket was strong today, with the All Ords finishing up 53 points due to a strong rise in the 20 leaders index. In America, the Dow Jones was flat but NASDAQ continued its strong run.

What does this all mean? We will come back to this news report at the end of the chapter.

This is where it is helpful to know how indices are constructed and what they are measuring.

A sharemarket index is a way of measuring the performance of a market over time. For instance, a sharemarket index tracks the change in value of a basket of shares over a period of time. The larger this basket of shares, the more the index represents the market as a whole. The Consumer Price Index is a well-known index; it measures the change in price of a basket of goods. Needless to say, the composition of the index basket and how each element in that basket is weighted are key features of an index.

Historically, the ASX calculated a variety of share price indices to help investors follow trends for particular industries or the sharemarket in general. The ASX All Ordinaries (or 'All Ords', as it is often referred to) was used as the main measure of how the Australian sharemarket was performing. Since April 2000, the S&P/ASX 200 has been used as the main market indicator.

The All Ords represents the 500 largest companies listed on the ASX. The index is rebalanced annually, with market capitalisation the only eligibility requirement. The index represents about ninety-five per cent of the Australian market.

There are two types of sharemarket indices:

¤   share price indices such as the All Ordinaries or S&P/ASX 200

¤   accumulation indices, which include dividends (such as the companion to the price index—the All Ordinaries Accumulation Index).

The accumulation index (also known as a total return index) takes into account reinvestment of dividends as well as capital value and therefore measures total return on investment. Calculation of the accumulation index assumes that the value of a company's dividend is reinvested across the whole index portfolio. If you hold a portfolio, this is probably the better benchmark to use because your share portfolio will most likely also have earned dividend income. This is especially so in Australia where companies have a history of paying higher dividends. Figure 9.1 shows a comparison between the All Ordinaries Index and the All Ordinaries Accumulation Index.

Figure 9.1: the All Ordinaries index versus the All Ordinaries Accumulation index

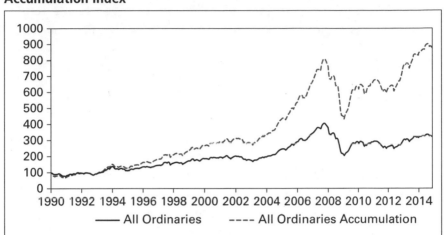

Standard & Poor's index services

The S&P/ASX indices are market-capitalisation weighted, with further adjustments for free float and liquidity to ensure investability. No adjustments are made in the All Ordinaries index for free float or liquidity.

Free float

Free float is defined by Standard & Poor's as 'the "contestable" shares of a company available in the marketplace'. Free float excludes parent holdings and government holdings from the index because these shares aren't regarded as generally available to investors. By excluding these shareholdings, the index seeks to better reflect the movement in price of the shareholdings that can be readily bought and sold.

As well as indices measuring the overall performance of the market, investors and fund managers are predominantly interested in how specific segments are faring. It can be a particular industry, just the largest companies or perhaps just the smaller companies on the market.

S&P/ASX 20™ and S&P/ASX 50™

The S&P/ASX 20 and S&P/ASX 50 represent, respectively, the top 20 and top 50 Australian companies listed on the Australian sharemarket by market capitalisation.

S&P/ASX 100™

The S&P/ASX 100 includes the top 100 companies by market capitalisation. The index provides a benchmark for large, active investment managers where the emphasis is on having a portfolio with sufficient liquidity. There is also an industrial and a resources S&P/ASX 100 which only includes those 100 companies whose activities qualify as industrial or resources.

S&P/ASX 200™

The S&P/ASX 200 contains the stocks represented by the S&P/ASX 100 plus the next 100 stocks selected on the basis of market capitalisation adjusted for free float and liquidity.

S&P/ASX 300™

The S&P/ASX 300 contains the stocks represented in the S&P/ASX 200 plus the next 100 stocks selected on the basis of market capitalisation adjusted for free float and liquidity.

The S&P/ASX Small Ordinaries Index

The S&P/ASX Australian Small Ordinaries Index comprises the smallest representatives of the S&P/ASX 300 Index. This index provides a benchmark for small-cap investments. The companies included in this index are companies included in the S&P/ASX 300 index but not in the S&P/ASX 100 index.

Other Australian indices

As well as the All Ordinaries and the various S&P indices, the Australian market is also divided into the various industry sector groupings. The sector indices are used to reflect the nature of the companies listed on the ASX. Standard & Poor's has introduced global sector indices to the Australian market that are derived from the Global Industry Classification (GICS) structure. Table 9.1 lists the sectors, with examples of companies within each sector.

Table 9.1: sector indices (as at 2014)

Industry group	Sample companies
Energy	Oil Search, Santos, Woodside Petroleum
Materials	Boral, Orica, Brickworks
Metals and Mining	BHP Billiton, Rio Tinto, Fortescue Metals Group
Gold (Metals and Mining sub-industry)	Newcrest Mining, Evolution Mining, OceanaGold
Industrials	Brambles, Leighton Holdings, Qantas
Consumer Discretionary	Fairfax Media, Domino's Pizza, Tabcorp
Consumer Staples	Woolworths, Bega Cheese, Tassal Group
Health Care	CSL, ResMed, Ramsay
Financials — ex Property Trusts	AMP, Westpac, CBA
Property Trusts	GPT Group, Stockland, Westfield
Information Technology	Computershare, IRESS Market Technology, carsales.com
Telecommunications Services	Telstra, TPG Telecom, M2 Group
Utilities	AGL Energy, Spark Infrastructure Group, Ausnet Services

Definitions of the industry groups are available on the ASX website (www.asx.com.au).

How S&P/ASX indices are calculated

The ASX website and Standard & Poor's have detailed information on how their indices are calculated, what changes have been made and other information not included here.

For our purposes, the most important thing to remember is that these indices are capitalisation weighted. They measure the change in the aggregate market value of the stocks in the basket so it follows that a 5-cent price movement in a large stock such as Telstra, BHP or one of the banks is going to have a bigger impact on the relevant index than a 5-cent movement in a much smaller company.

Your portfolio versus the index

You may come across the term 'beta'. Beta is a sensitivity measure of stock price volatility relative to a broad market index. Some share portfolios have a high correlation to the performance of a broader market. Those portfolios would be said to have a high beta. Other portfolios may seek to track a different index.

Depending on the composition of your portfolio, it may have a high correlation to the performance of a broader market or it may not. If you have a portfolio of large capitalisation market leaders you would expect to have a higher beta than if you have a portfolio of smaller stocks.

So when you hear a report of a significant rise or fall in the market, this may be due to movement in the price of a few large stocks because of their high weighting in the index. Your portfolio may have been unaffected or moved in the opposite direction.

International indices

Indices are used to benchmark sharemarkets all around the world, with the most well-known being the United States' Dow Jones Industrial Average (DJIA). This is a share price index that measures the market prices of 30 companies listed on the New York Stock Exchange. Unlike the Australian share price indices, each stock in the Dow is price weighted rather than capitalisation weighted. The name implies manufacturing, but the basket of stocks is more diverse than this; it includes pharmaceutical companies, technology companies and investment banks, to name a few. The smaller number of stocks in the Dow means that the Standard & Poor's 500

(S&P 500) better reflects the broader economy. For a measure of the performance of technology companies, investors generally refer to the NASDAQ indices as NASDAQ has many technology companies listed on its market.

In London, the Financial Times Stock Exchange Index, better known as the FTSE 100, closely corresponds to the S&P 500 and the All Ordinaries. The FTSE (or 'Footsie') lists the 100 largest public companies traded on the London Stock Exchange.

Other major markets include the Hong Kong, Japanese and German markets. The Hang Seng is the principal Hong Kong share price index. The main market barometer in Japan is the Nikkei Dow Index, which covers the top 225 shares listed on the Tokyo Stock Exchange. The German Stock Exchange, Dax 30 (covering the top 30 German-listed stocks), is unusual in that it is an accumulation index, whereas all the others are price indices, meaning they do not include income (dividends).

Sharemarket analysis using indices

Investors look at the past performance shown in the sharemarket indices in an attempt to determine where the market will go in the future. They also use indices as a comparison with the performance of their own sharemarket portfolio. However, great care needs to be taken when using sharemarket indices as a guide to future performance, and also when making comparisons with the past, as the composition of the indices often changes over time.

For example, the Dow Jones celebrated its hundredth birthday a few years ago. Of all the companies originally included in the index when it was formed, only one stock, the General Electric Company, remained in the index a century later.

Careful scrutiny is also necessary when comparing indices from one country to another as there may be different rules regarding the composition of a particular index and how it is calculated.

Index movements

Daily index movements are more meaningful when understood in percentage terms. For example, assuming the All Ordinaries is at 6000 points, a 100-point gain represents a 1.7 per cent rise; on the Dow Jones Index, however, a 100-point gain is a gain of only 0.8 per cent (assuming the Dow Jones is at 13 000 points).

Upward trend

In general, there is an upward trend in the value of shares listed on the Australian Securities Exchange (ASX). However, the price of shares in any one company largely reflects the year-to-year performance of that company. Share prices overall are also affected by general economic conditions and market sentiment.

You should be mindful of a few things when looking at a chart of the market and observing a long-term upward trend:

¤ Indices of this type have an upward bias. Why? Well, consider what happens when a company shrinks below the minimum capitalisation (price X shares on issue) required for inclusion in the index or if a company goes broke — the company is taken out of the index and a different company is included, so over time, the poorer performing companies get weeded out.

¤ It is one thing to see the long-term upward trend, but if you buy on a peak and then, for whatever reason, sell when the market has fallen back you will not be participating in the uptrend.

¤ The indices measuring the performance of companies listed on the ASX are capitalisation weighted indices, which means that a given movement in price for a large company will have more impact on the index than the same price movement for smaller companies in the index. So, for example, if the big four banks all have a good day / bad day that will have a big impact on moving the index up/down even though a lot of smaller companies may have fallen/risen in price that day.

¤ While the overall market may be trending upwards, it doesn't necessarily mean that the shares in your portfolio will replicate the uptrend (that is, the beta — the correlation between price movements in your share/s versus the overall market).

Let's have a look at table 9.2, which lists all the companies that were added to or deleted from the All Ordinaries Index in 2013 and 2014. There's a few there you might recognise as once being very popular stocks but eventually, either due to corporate actions or as their fortunes declined they no longer met the criteria for continued inclusion in the index. And of course there are some companies that dropped out of the index for a period only to be re-included later on as their circumstances changed.

Table 9.2: companies added to and deleted from the All Ordinaries Index in 2013 and 2014

	Added		Removed	
Year	Company name	Ticker	Company name	Ticker
2014	APN News & Media Ltd	APN	Medusa Mining Limited	MML
2014	Vocus Communications Limited	VOC	Resolute Mining Ltd	RSG
2014	Healthscope Ltd	HSO	Wotif.com Holdings	WTF
2014	Asaleo Care Ltd	AHY	Buru Energy Limited	BRU
2014	Liquefied Natural Gas Limited	LNG	NRW Holdings Limited	NWH
2014	Technology One Ltd	TNE	The Reject Shop Limited	TRS
2014	Genworth Mortgage Insurance Australia Limited	GMA	Australand Property Group	ALZ
2014	Spotless Group Holdings Ltd	SPO	Envestra Ltd	ENV
2014	Greencross Ltd	GXL	David Jones Ltd	DJS
2014	Japara Healthcare Limited	JHC	Aquila Resources	AQA
2014	Tassal Group Limited	TGR	Acrux Ltd	ACR
2014	Steadfast Group Limited	SDF	Aurora Oil & Gas Ltd	AUT
2014	Sundance Energy Australia Ltd	SEA	21st Century Fox Inc	FOX
2014	ARB Corp Ltd	ARP	Alacer Gold Corp.	AQG
2014	Ainsworth Game Technology Ltd	AGI	Ausdrill Ltd	ASL
2014	Bega Cheese Ltd	BGA	Decmil Group Ltd	DCG
2014	Cover-more Group Ltd	CVO	Energy World Corporation Ltd	EWC

(continued)

Table 9.2: companies added to and deleted from the All Ordinaries Index in 2013 and 2014 *(cont'd)*

	Added		Removed	
Year	Company name	Ticker	Company name	Ticker
2014	OzForex Group Limited	OFX	SMS Management & Technology Ltd	SMX
2014	Pact Group Ltd	PGH	Silver Lake Resources Ltd	SLR
2014	Veda Group Limited	VED	Virgin Australia Holdings Ltd	VAH
2014	Aveo Group Trust	AOG	Commonwealth Property Office	CPA
2014	Nine Entertainment Co. Holdings Limited	NEC	Forge Group Ltd	FGE
2013	BC Iron Limited	BCI	Boart Longyear Limited	BLY
2013	Retail Food Group Limited	RFG	Cudeco Limited	CDU
2013	SkyCity Entertainment Group	SKC	Fleetwood Corp Ltd	FWD
2013	Slater & Gordon Limited	SGH	Kingsgate Consolidated Ltd	KCN
2013	Village Roadshow Ltd	VRL	OceanaGold Corporation - CDI	OGC
2013	Virtus Health Limited	VRT	Perseus Mining Limited	PRU
2013	Orora Limited	ORA	St Barbara Limited	SBM
2013	Recall Holdings Limited	REC	Sundance Resources Limited	SDL
2013	Kathmandu Holdings Limited	KMD	Linc Energy	LNC
2013	Cromwell Property Group	CMW	Billabong Intl Ltd	BBG
2013	Forge Group Ltd	FGE	Discovery Metals Ltd	DML
2013	STW Communications Group Ltd	SGN	Emeco Holdings	EHL
2013	Sky Network Television Limited	SKT	FKP Property Group	FKP
2013	Automotive Holdings Group Ltd	AHE	Mineral Deposits Limited	MDL
2013	Domino's Pizza Enterprises Ltd	DMP	Australian Infrastructure Fund Limited	AIX
2013	G8 Education Limited	GEM	Coalspur Mines Ltd	CPL
2013	Linc Energy	LNC	Imdex Limited	IMD
2013	REA Group Ltd	REA	Maverick Drilling & Exploration Ltd.	MAD

Year	Added Company name	Ticker	Removed Company name	Ticker
2013	Sirius Resources NL	SIR	Mirabela Nickel Limited	MBN
2013	New Newscorp Inc	NNC	Troy Resources Limited	TRY
2013	Horizon Oil Ltd	HZN	Bathurst Resources Limited	BTU
2013	Magellan Financial Group Limited	MFG	Gindalbie Metals Ltd	GBG
2013	Premier Investments Ltd	PMV	Gryphon Minerals Ltd	GRY
2013	Trade Me Ltd	TME	Saracen Mineral Holdings Ltd	SAR

Having read the information on indices, let's now revisit the news report.

> After a slow start, turnover on the sharemarket was strong today, with the All Ords finishing up 53 points due to a strong rise in the 20 leaders index. In America, the Dow Jones was flat but NASDAQ continued its strong run.

A simple reading of this report would be that although the Australian market went up, it was the high capitalisation market leaders that pushed it up and other companies may not have performed similarly. In the United States, the big, mature companies listed on the NYSE did not do much, but the technology companies that tend to list on NASDAQ are on an uptrend.

*   *   *

Some people find investing in individual companies too challenging. Others have a specific aim of getting broad exposure without having to buy a lot of different securities. For these investors managed funds can often meet their need — and there are a lot choose from.

CHAPTER 10

Managed funds

So far in this book we have talked about buying and selling shares directly—that is, doing your own research, making your own decisions and investing in companies in your own name.

However, there is another option—you can use the services of a professional investment organisation that pools your money with other investors' money and makes the investment decisions for you. This investment option is called a managed fund.

Managed funds are a popular and relatively easy way to invest. One transaction gives you access to a range of investments, across different asset classes, market sectors and investments that may otherwise be out of reach—such as shopping centres, office blocks, international shares and small-cap stocks or emerging markets.

Managed funds enable you to access a diversified portfolio made up of different asset classes and industry sectors. This can help manage your level of investment risk by minimising the impact of poor performance by a particular industry or industry sector.

What are managed funds?

Managed funds pool the money of individual investors. The combined capital is invested by a professional fund manager. Depending on the fund manager's mandate, investments can be made across a range of asset classes such as shares, bonds and property, as well as infrastructure assets.

When you invest in a managed fund, you are allocated a number of shares or units in the fund. Each share or unit represents an equal portion of the fund's value. You may receive regular payments—called dividends or distributions—from the fund, based on the profit or income it receives from the underlying investments.

Your profit potential is a combination of any income you receive plus capital gains from selling the units at a price higher than your purchase price.

Why use managed funds?

Choice, flexibility and ease of use are key reasons to consider a managed fund.

Managed funds offer choice—choice of asset class to invest in, choice of level of risk, choice of investment manager and choice of how you buy and sell them.

Flexibility comes from the variety of access options. You can buy managed funds either directly from the fund manager—that is, off market. Other managed funds are available to trade on ASX just like shares. In addition, there is a hybrid approach—the mFund service—which enables you to purchase a fund's units from the manager, while using the ASX settlement system to facilitate the process.

Because a fund manager is making the investment decisions for you, once you have decided which fund to invest in, owning a managed fund is a relatively simple activity.

Drawbacks of managed funds

You will be charged a fee for investing in a managed fund. This fee is charged regardless of the success of the fund. Some funds will charge an additional fee if the fund manager outperforms a benchmark. The more complicated or hard to access the assets in which the fund invests, the higher the fund fees are likely to be. Fees are typically expressed as an annual percentage of the total amount you have invested. For example, a 1.5 per cent per annum fee would mean that if you invested $10 000 your fee would be $150 for the year. Be aware that funds can have entry and exit fees too, so make sure you read the fine print.

Investing in a managed fund introduces a new variable into your decision making—the skill of the fund manager. The choices made by the fund manager in an actively managed fund will have a major outcome on the investment. Even the most skilful fund manager is not immune to broad market downturns that drag on markets. Given this, it makes sense to have a good understanding of the stated investment strategy of the fund as well as the investing experience of the fund manager. All reputable managed funds have this set out clearly on their website and in their fund documents.

The fine print

As with all investment decisions, it is essential that you fully understand what you are investing in. The more complicated the fund, the harder it may be for you to understand the circumstances under which you could lose money.

The managed fund family

While choice can be a benefit, it can also be an added complication. The term 'managed fund' covers an extremely broad range of investment options. To make sense of the landscape, it can help to identify some key characteristics of managed funds, namely:

¤ the assets they offer exposure to

¤ how they are bought and sold

¤   their legal structures (What's in a name?)

¤   active and passive funds.

Asset exposure

Australian shares

There is a wide variety of managed funds that provide exposure to the Australian sharemarket. Most of the managed funds seek to outperform the return of the relevant index by investing directly in a subset of the securities included in the index or benchmark.

There are also managed funds targeting exposure to a particular sector or sectors of the market. Investors can also access strategy-oriented managed funds such as high-dividend funds, value-focused funds or those with a bias towards large or small capitalisation stocks.

Income earned by a fund, including franking credits, can be distributed back to investors, most typically on a semi-annual basis.

International shares

International managed funds can assist investors to diversify into overseas markets while also diversifying across companies within those international markets.

International managed funds can be single country (for example, China), multi-country within the same region (for example, Europe) or multi-region (for example, emerging markets). There are also international sector-managed funds available that may assist investors to access sectors (such as technology) which are underrepresented within the Australian market.

International managed funds may or may not be hedged against currency movements and may also include additional taxation requirements. Investors should review the risks associated with international managed funds before investing.

Fixed income

Fixed-income managed funds are issued over a basket of bonds which, depending on the fund's mandate, can include a variety of domestic and international corporates, Australian Commonwealth, State and Territory governments, government treasury corporations, semi-government entities and international governments. Typically, the underlying fund will have a variety of bonds with varying maturity dates and as one bond matures, it will be replaced by another, to ensure there is sufficient diversity in the portfolio being tracked.

Fixed-income managed funds can help investors access a more reliable income stream with typically less price volatility than other classes such as shares. This is why investing in this asset class is often referred to as 'defensive'. A fixed-income managed fund will usually distribute the income earned on a quarterly basis.

Balanced

Balanced managed funds are issued over a range of asset classes including Australian and international shares, fixed income, property and cash. Typically, the aim of these funds is to provide a mixture of capital growth and/or income over the medium to long term.

Balanced funds can help you achieve diversification across asset classes when you have smaller amounts to invest.

Buying and selling

Managed funds can be split between those that you can buy and sell on ASX (listed managed funds) and those that are traded off-market (unlisted managed funds). The mFund settlement service enables you to buy unlisted funds via the same broker you use to transact shares and to have your holdings recorded alongside all your other holdings in CHESS.

Unlisted funds

Unlisted managed funds are the most common type of managed fund available to Australian investors.

Buy and sell prices for units in unlisted funds are decided by the fund manager and are typically based on the most recent valuation of fund assets. These prices are usually available from the fund's website or published in national newspapers.

There is an administrative process for buying and selling, which means it will take longer to complete the process than buying on-market.

mFunds

The mFund settlement service was developed to address the delays in the transaction process and improve the transparency of unit prices for unlisted managed funds.

More detailed information is available from the ASX website; however, in simple terms, the service operates as follows.

Unlisted funds sign up for the mFund settlement service. Buy and sell prices for units in approved funds are displayed online. Being 'unlisted' means that they are not directly traded on ASX. Instead, purchases and sales of units in the fund are made between the investor and the managed fund issuer's unit registry. Investors do not trade units with other investors; rather, the process is facilitated by the ASX settlement system, CHESS.

However, you can transact in these units via your broker as you would with shares. A major convenience for investors is that the process is entirely online and the holding in unlisted funds that you have bought via the mFunds settlement service will appear in your CHESS holding statements alongside your other CHESS holdings. When you sell your holding the CHESS statement will change accordingly.

Listed managed funds

ASX offers listed managed funds that include:

¤ listed investment companies (LICs) and trusts (LITs)

¤ A-REITs (Australian real estate investment trusts)

¤ infrastructure funds

¤ absolute return funds

¤ pooled development funds.

Listed investment companies

Listed managed funds may have similar mandates and even the same fund managers as some unlisted funds, but all buying and selling is done on-market and the bid and offer prices are those of actual investors wanting to buy and sell. Consequently, the market prices will reflect the value of the assets held by the fund but will also reflect market sentiment for that fund, for the assets the fund has invested in, for the managed fund sector and for the market overall. For this reason ASX listed managed funds can trade at a price above or below their asset backing. Unlisted funds, on the other hand, may usually be purchased and redeemed at their net tangible asset backing.

Unlike unlisted funds, listed managed funds are bought and sold on-market. This means you are not redeeming your units with the fund manager and they do not need to sell any of the fund's assets to pay you.

A-REITs

A-REITs enable investors to buy an interest in a professionally managed and diversified portfolio of commercial real estate. Investors gain exposure to both the value of the real estate the trust owns and the regular rental income generated from the properties. These investments may include the following:

- office buildings
- industrial estates
- retail shopping centres
- hotels and entertainment precincts
- overseas properties.

The fund manager selects the investment properties and is responsible for all maintenance, administration, rentals and improvements.

Infrastructure funds

Infrastructure funds enable investors to own a part of a professionally managed portfolio of infrastructure assets, such as:

- toll roads
- airports
- communications assets

⌧   materials-handling facilities such as docks

⌧   rail facilities and other transport assets

⌧   utilities such as electricity power lines and gas pipelines.

Returns from infrastructure funds may have a combination of capital growth and income. The incomes generated by infrastructure assets may be predictable as they usually operate in environments with low levels of competition and high barriers to entry.

Absolute return funds

Absolute return (or hedge) funds are managed funds that aim to produce returns in both rising and falling markets. The investment techniques adopted by an absolute return fund may vary from methods employed by a traditional fund manager. Rather than the traditional 'buy and hold' approach, absolute return funds have greater scope to use sophisticated trading strategies to try to benefit from opportunities in the market.

Pooled development funds

Pooled development funds (PDFs) were established through the *Pooled Development Act (1992)* to encourage investment in small and medium-sized Australian companies. PDFs invest in shares of small to medium Australian companies with assets of less than $50 million.

Because these companies are normally in the formative stage of development, most PDFs are generally considered to be higher risk investments. Shareholders in PDFs don't pay income tax on earnings or capital gains tax if holdings are sold at a profit. Equally, capital gains losses are not tax deductible.

Exchange-traded products

Exchange-traded products (ETPs) is the family name for the group of products comprising exchange-traded funds (ETFs), managed funds (MFs) and structured products (SPs). They are very popular overseas, especially in the United States, and are proving increasingly popular here because of the range of assets they can provide exposure to with relatively low management fees. A list of ETPs is available on the ASX website. It is a long list and it continues to grow. Because of the growing interest and evolving nature of this market segment we are going to go into a bit more detail.

ETPs are open-ended, which means that the number of units on issue is not fixed but can increase or decrease in response to demand and supply from investors. This assists in ensuring that the ETPs trade at or near their net asset value (NAV). ETPs trade, clear and settle in the same way as shares on the ASX.

They offer exposure to:

¤ Australian equities

¤ international equities

¤ commodities

¤ fixed income

¤ currencies

¤ cash rates.

An investor could conceivably obtain a balanced portfolio and switch between asset classes using ETPs exclusively.

Creation and redemption

Various factors cause ETPs to revert to trading at net asset value. If there is strong demand, issuers can increase supply by issuing more units, which will prevent market prices rising above net asset value (NAV). Conversely, if market prices go to a discount to NAV, the issuer and other approved institutional investors can buy back units and convert them into the underlying assets. So if an ETP starts to trade at below the NAV an arbitrage profit becomes available in buying the ETF units and then redeeming them for the underlying assets, which are worth more. Thus arbitrage will cause any discount to be relatively short-lived.

Buying and selling ETPs

The ETP market operates a bit differently from the market for shares. Investors typically look at a market for a security before they invest. They look at the bid and offer spread and the volume — daily, weekly or monthly. Some investors get put off when they see relatively low volume for some ETPs. Accordingly, they conclude that the instruments are illiquid and best avoided. But the ETP market operates a bit differently from ordinary shares.

First up, you can expect 'natural' buying and selling volume to be relatively low because ETFs are a buy-and-hold instrument. To provide liquidity, ETP issuers, or their agents, provide an important role in ensuring that buyers and sellers of ETPs can transact. They provide liquidity to the market by providing quotes through the trading day and they update their prices to reflect changes in the underlying securities. If there is no market when you place an order to buy or to sell a certain quantity you should expect a market maker to respond quickly. If your order is likely to be large, your broker may contact the market makers in advance.

It may be prudent to delay your trading until after all the stocks in the market have opened as this gives ETP market makers an opportunity to establish current values. Confining your buying and selling to between 10.30 am and 3.30 pm Sydney time would be prudent.

You may now ask 'How do I know what the right price is?' Issuers are required to disclose the net asset value so you will know the market you can expect—give or take. Some report this figure to the market; others post it on their website.

What's in a name? Legal structures

We need to cover some technical matters. There has been a lot of debate in the industry and with regulators about how these various instruments should be named and characterised. The concern about lumping them all under the same label is that this may suggest they are all 'built' the same and your legal rights as a holder may be the same—but they are not. Different products that may appear to offer similar investment outcomes have different names because they are structured differently.

Exchange traded funds (ETFs) and managed funds (MFs) are typically registered managed investment schemes (MIS). Investors in an ETP structured as a managed investment scheme hold units in a unit trust rather than shares in a company that operates the investment fund. Each unit represents an interest in a portfolio of assets held by the ETP.

Structured Products (SPs), however, typically represent contractual obligations of the issuer so investors may not receive an interest in the portfolio of assets held by the SP but instead rely on rights against the issuer. In the case of ETFs you obtain your exposure by holding units in the company that operates the fund. In the case of SPs you hold an instrument that contracts the issuer to provide you with the exposure.

ETFs are typically passive index tracking investments and in most instances are either physically backed or adopt a representative sampling approach, which means they include enough of the underlying asset to achieve the performance of the underlying index without necessarily replicating the underlying index portfolio. Alternatively, ETF issuers may choose to replicate synthetically the performance of the assets that they seek to track. Such ETFs can carry specific risks and would be identified as they are required to have the word 'synthetic' as part of their naming convention.

Structured products typically do not invest in the underlying securities/ assets but rather they aim to replicate the performance of the index or benchmark synthetically. There can be many reasons why product issuers choose the synthetic replication approach. For example, it may be impractical to invest and hold a physical security when the underlying security is a commodity such as wheat or oil.

Synthetics

Synthetic replication is done by holding financial instruments, most likely a futures contract, to simulate the investment performance of the index or benchmark for the whole fund.

Synthetic ETPs and SPs use derivatives to achieve their investment objective. If you invest in these you are subject to the risk that the counterparty to the derivative may fail to meet some or all of its obligations. This risk applies to the portion of the synthetic ETPs or SPs assets that represents money owing under the derivatives. This risk is greater when the issuer uses over the counter (OTC) derivatives that are not subject to central counterparty clearing arrangements. Typically, most synthetic ETP issuers use OTC swap contracts that are not subject to central counterparty clearing.

To assist in mitigating this counterparty risk, ASX requires that each synthetic ETF be operated to keep the amount of assets reflecting money owing by OTC derivative counterparties to a limit of up to 10 per cent of the net asset value (NAV) of the ETF. If for some reason the counterparty fails to meet its obligations to the ETF, the fund may not be able to deliver its return objective and investors could lose up to 10 per cent or more of the value of their investment in the ETF.

Additionally, the ASX has mandated that all derivative counterparties for synthetic ETFs on the ASX must meet certain eligibility requirements to minimise the risk of the counterparty failing to perform.

Active and passive funds

Another differentiator in the managed fund family is whether the fund is passive or active. Active funds seek to outperform a benchmark by the fund manager using their nous to decide what to invest in. The fund's mandate dictates what the manager can and can't invest in, but beyond that it may actively manage its holdings.

A typical example of a passive fund is an index fund. It does not seek to outperform a benchmark; it seeks to replicate the performance of a benchmark index by having the fund replicate, or closely approximate, the holdings in the index and their weightings.

The majority of ETFs fall into the passive, or index fund, camp. A benefit of ETFs is the lower management fees they tend to offer compared to actively managed funds.

Active products

Managed funds, which are considered part of the ETP family, can include actively managed as well as passively managed forms of investments. These managed funds can be constructed to achieve a certain outcome, such as funds designed to generate returns that are negatively correlated to the returns of the Australian sharemarket (as measured by the S&P/ASX 200 index).

As a rule of thumb, the more active the manager is in maintaining the asset mix needed to achieve the stated performance objective, the higher you can expect the fees—also known as the management expense ratio (MER)—to be.

*   *   *

If you have read this far, we hope you are growing in confidence about getting into the sharemarket. If you do start investing and find you enjoy it and are getting more confident you might be thinking, 'What's next?' For confident investors, gearing is a strategy to look at for boosting profits, and we cover this in chapter 11.

Gearing and margin lending

The author acknowledges and appreciates the contribution provided by Bendigo and Adelaide Bank's margin lending division (Leveraged Equities) in the preparation of this chapter.

Gearing (or leverage) is an investment strategy for getting exposure to an asset with a smaller amount of capital than would be required to buy the asset outright. 'Exposure' can mean different things depending on the asset. For financial assets such as shares, exposure generally means the right to earn any income and capital returns on the asset. There are many ways to implement a gearing strategy and one common way is to borrow part of the purchase price of an asset—for example, borrowing part of the purchase price of an investment property.

The reason gearing magnifies gains and losses is simple mathematics. Let's say an asset's price is $100. You acquire the asset with $20 of your own capital and borrow $80. The asset then increases in value and you sell it for $110. After repaying the loan you are left with $30, which is $10 more than your original investment, or a gain of 50 per cent on your $20 investment (ignoring interest, taxes and fees).

In this example, the asset's price increased by 10 per cent but you earned a return of 50 per cent on your own capital—gearing magnified your exposure to the asset's returns. The converse is also true. If you sell the asset for $90, after repaying the loan you will be left with only $10, which is half your original $20 investment.

Investors who gear by borrowing will incur interest on the loan. If the investors (who are Australian taxpayers) acquire an income-producing asset, they can usually claim an income tax deduction for the loan interest.

Investors may be able to select an investment that pays a dividend or income that is greater than the loan interest. This is called positive gearing. When the periodic income or dividend earned on the investment is less than the loan interest, this is called negative gearing.

For any gearing strategy you should bear in mind a few key points:

¤ Consider total returns and the costs of gearing on an after-tax basis.

¤ The gearing strategy should 'capture' both forms of returns— income and capital growth. Generally, this means dividends or investment income should be used to offset any loan interest, or reduce the amount borrowed or reinvested.

¤ How much you should gear will depend on your financial objectives and your ability to recover capital losses if markets fall. And it also depends on your expectations about investment returns relative to interest rates. At a minimum, if you don't believe the asset will make sufficient after-tax total returns to cover the after-tax costs of borrowing, you should not gear and maybe not invest at all.

¤ Any investment decision must start with your goals and circumstances. If you decide to gear by borrowing to acquire an asset you then have two interrelated decisions: how much to borrow and what to invest in. Never borrow beyond your ability to meet the repayments.

The risk of losing more capital

When you gear, you increase the potential of losing a greater amount of capital than you otherwise would.

You could buy stocks X, Y and Z outright or you may decide to gear to get more exposure to those companies. The risk of investing in those companies is the same, but when you gear you have more money invested in those stocks, even if some of that money is not your own! Also, if you buy the shares outright and they then fall in value, you can hold onto them and hope they recover (although they may fall further). But if you buy the shares on margin and the shares fall enough to trigger a margin call (more on this later in the chapter) you will be required to put in additional funds or sell some of the holding. If it is the latter, you will be selling into an already falling market that may not suit your circumstances or view of the market.

Given all this it should be clear that you should not gear by borrowing to invest unless you:

¤ believe the investment asset is expected to earn a total return greater than the costs of borrowing (on an after-tax basis)

¤ understand and are prepared to accept the risks, including a loss of your capital

¤ have the financial resources to recover if you do experience a loss.

Margin loans

A margin loan is a facility that enables you to borrow part of the capital needed to buy various assets including Australian listed shares, exchange traded funds and managed funds. The investment portfolio you acquire becomes the collateral for your loan. This is in contrast to a redraw facility on a home loan, for example, where the home is the collateral for the loan. You can also use an existing portfolio of acceptable financial assets as collateral for borrowing money to acquire other investments—should you want to diversify your investments, for example. Importantly, you are the registered owner of your investments (except in a few circumstances such as a corporate takeover) and except in the event of a default, you control what happens to those investments and are entitled to all the returns.

Unlike a traditional loan, the periodic repayments on a margin loan are interest only and there is no fixed time by which you must repay the principal. This means you can maintain a gearing strategy for the length of time that suits your circumstances and expectations about the portfolio's capital growth.

The investment portfolio is divisible. If your circumstances change, it is possible to sell a proportion of an investment portfolio to reduce the loan. Compare this to trying to sell only half a house to reduce a mortgage.

As with any loan, the application process for a margin loan typically involves submitting financial details to the lender as well as evidence of your ability to meet the interest payments (such as pay slips, for example). The lender will then assess whether to approve your loan and the approval can generally be completed within a few days, depending on your circumstances. Most margin lenders have a minimum loan amount — usually $20 000 — although it may be possible to apply for a smaller loan.

The maximum amount you may be able to borrow depends on:

¤   the credit limit the margin lender approves

¤   the amount the lender will allow you to borrow against your investment portfolio. This is expressed as a percentage of the market value of your investment portfolio and is called the loan-to-value ratio or LVR

¤   the market value of your investment value.

Most margin lenders offer LVRs of between 50 per cent and 75 per cent. For example, blue chip shares will usually have an LVR of 75 per cent. This means you can borrow $75 to acquire a $100 investment, with the remaining $25 being contributed by you. More speculative small cap shares may have a lower LVR of, say, 60 per cent, whereas a managed fund that includes a diversified portfolio of quality shares may have a higher LVR of, say, 75 per cent. Each lender publishes a list of acceptable investments and the LVR that applies to each investment. The margin lender may periodically add or remove acceptable investments or change the LVR that applies to a given investment.

Most investors take the prudent approach and borrow much less than the maximum amount the lender will allow. For example, you may acquire a portfolio of blue chip shares by borrowing only half of the purchase price. In this case, your gearing ratio is 50 per cent (you borrow $50 and contribute $50 of your own capital to acquire a $100 portfolio) even though the lender may have an LVR of 75 per cent.

It is important to remember that your gearing ratio constantly changes. As the market value of your investment portfolio goes up, your gearing ratio goes down. Conversely, as the market value of your investment portfolio goes down, your gearing ratio goes up.

Margin call

A margin call is an urgent demand by the lender for you to reduce your gearing ratio to an acceptable level. A margin call can be triggered by the market value of your investment portfolio falling, thus increasing your gearing ratio. An acceptable level means reducing your gearing ratio to no more than the LVR set by the lender for your investment portfolio.

A margin call is only triggered when your gearing ratio exceeds the LVR plus a buffer. The lender sets a buffer to avoid triggering a margin call for every small market fluctuation. Margin lenders typically offer buffers of 5 per cent or 10 per cent. For example, if the LVR for your portfolio is 75 per cent and there is a 10 per cent buffer, a margin call will be triggered when your gearing ratio exceeds 85 per cent. It is important to recognise that if you do receive a margin call you must return your gearing ratio to below the LVR. You can't just bring your gearing back to just below the 'LVR plus buffer' amount — it must come back below the LVR.

If you do receive a margin call, most margin lenders only allow you 24 hours to take action. To rectify your margin loan you can either:

- sell some of your investment portfolio and use the sale proceeds to reduce the loan amount
- use cash from other accounts to reduce the loan amount
- add other acceptable investments to the margin loan facility to increase the value of the investment portfolio accepted by the margin lender.

The right approach to take will depend on your circumstances and market expectations. If you believe the value of the investment portfolio will continue to fall, then selling, even at a loss, may be preferable to losing even more capital. In contrast, if you believe the fall in value is only temporary, you may prefer to reduce the loan amount using other available cash.

A margin call can have serious consequences. If you fail to take appropriate action, the lender has the right to sell some of or your entire investment portfolio. Successful investors take a disciplined approach, particularly when gearing. They monitor their portfolio and make adjustments well before a margin call becomes a reality. In addition they are conscious of a natural behavioural bias against realising losses, even when it is financially sensible to sell. In other words, we are often reluctant to sell if it means crystallising a loss, but sometimes cutting your losses is the more sensible thing to do.

Assume the portfolio has a loan-to-value ratio (LVR) of 75 per cent and a buffer of 10 per cent. A margin call occurs when the gearing ratio is above 85 per cent, as shown in table 11.1.

Table 11.1: how a margin call works

	Start	'In the buffer' (no margin call)	Margin call
Loan	$50 000	$50 000	$50 000
Portfolio value	$83 000	$63 000 A fall of about 24% from starting value.	$58 000 A fall of about 30% from starting value.
Gearing ratio (loan divided by portfolio value)	60%	79%	86% The loan must be reduced by $6500 or the portfolio increased by $25 000.

Buying shares via a margin loan facility

You will be paying for your shares via your margin loan so the purchase of those shares needs to be linked to your margin loan. Although some margin lenders may be closely affiliated with a certain broker, you are not obligated to trade through any particular broker. Buying and selling shares via your margin loan can be an automated process or it may involve a manual process where the broker contacts the margin lender to ensure you have the available credit before placing the order. In the latter case, this may mean you will be asked to pay higher brokerage. You should discuss with your margin lender or your broker what is the most convenient and cost-effective option for you.

Double gearing

'Double gearing' can have different meanings:

¤ It can be used to describe borrowing from a home loan and using that money as the capital contribution for a margin loan.

¤ It can also mean borrowing to acquire an asset that is itself geared—for example, a managed fund that uses gearing within the fund.

In the first case, the key issue is excessive gearing—borrowing too much relative to the total value of your assets. In the second case, the key issue is price volatility. As outlined above, gearing magnifies the impact of small market movements (both up and down). Thus, an investment with internal gearing will typically exhibit higher price volatility (on a given day, the price of the investment moves within a wide range, either up or down). Volatile investments are more likely (relative to investments that exhibit low price volatility) to fall in value by an amount sufficient to trigger a margin call.

What to avoid

People typically get into trouble with margin loans if:

¤ they gear highly and do not have a plan for responding to a margin call

¤ they do not monitor their loan and portfolio and respond as market expectations change, thus allowing their gearing ratio to move outside an acceptable range

¤ they concentrate their portfolio in too few assets so that a fall in price for one or two of those assets has a big impact on their portfolio's value

¤ they invest in very volatile assets which may go up rapidly but are also at risk of falling rapidly, thus potentially triggering a margin call.

* * *

It's one thing to have the tools; it's another to know what you're going to do with them. In the preceding chapters we have talked you through what you will encounter when investing in the sharemarket. Now it's time to turn our minds to applying that knowledge.

PART II
Making informed decisions—strategies and approaches to investing

Part II of this book looks at the benefits of adopting a share trading strategy. It will give you the tools and information to identify investment opportunities.

CHAPTER 12

Why you need a strategy

If you are going to invest in shares directly, you need to have a strategy. Your strategy should reflect your own circumstances, responsibilities and tolerance for risk. Your professional adviser can help you in developing this strategy—and you should seek independent financial advice from your adviser before making investment decisions.

A strategy can be thought of as a set of rules or guidelines that are adhered to consistently over time.

The strategy is always the focal point—and remember: it is not really a strategy if you don't adhere to it. But having a strategy does not preclude you from losses and it is during periods of adversity that your ability to stick to your strategy will be tested.

This chapter provides some insights into the mindset required to follow the strategy that you have adopted. The key to having the right mindset is understanding how important time (especially a longer term perspective), consistency, discipline and patience are to successful investing. Such an understanding will help you to disregard short-term volatility and take a more objective, consistently rational approach to wealth creation.

You will also see that by having your own focused strategy you can diversify your investments more effectively—with the objective of improving overall returns, rather than simply diversifying for its own sake.

Time and volatility

Markets can go through periods of quiet when prices tend to not move much at all. At other times the market can be very volatile, with significant price movement up or down even on a daily basis. When markets experience periods of significant short-term volatility it can be very unsettling to investors, perhaps causing them to question their chosen investment strategy. This can be particularly so for novice investors who have not seen market cycles play out and have not acquired the discipline of seasoned investors.

Your investment returns will typically be less volatile over the longer term and by focusing on your longer term objectives you can better avoid making rash decisions as a result of short-term price fluctuations.

Speculation

Speculation can be described as the taking of relatively large risks in the expectation of making relatively large gains in the short term. Often it involves taking advantage quickly of what are seen as short-term trading opportunities.

While limited speculation with the right tools and risk-management techniques can be profitable, and even fun, it should not dominate the investment strategy of most investors. By limiting the role of speculation, spectacular losses are less likely to undermine your long-term wealth-creation goals.

Dividends

Dividends can contribute to making your overall investment return less volatile. A portfolio that includes some well-selected higher yielding stocks may provide for steady or increased dividend payments over time, which will contribute to your overall return.

Rates of return over time

The rate of return you achieve with your investments is going to be affected significantly by when you enter the market. The return on an investment that was bought during a downturn in the market will probably be significantly higher than if the same assets are bought during a market peak.

Of course, it is easy to say that it is best to buy assets when their price is low because the return will be higher than if you buy those assets when their price is high. But you need to have confidence that their price will in fact recover if it is low. Also of importance to note is that a company may be categorised as 'expensive' but its shares still continue to rise in price over the following years due to the quality of the company.

There are two points to remember. First, beware of rates of return if you do not know the starting and end points, particularly when comparing rates of return.

Second, if you are confident in the investments you want to make, your investment return will be helped considerably if you can time your purchase rather than rushing in during a market peak. It is rare for a company's share to not pull back at some time for some reason. It could be part of a general market correction, there may be profit taking that causes the price to recede or there may be some market news that alarms investors even though the fundamentals remain very strong. This is sometimes referred to as a period of temporary weakness and you may see broker recommendations to 'buy on weakness'. It is often recommended when a stock has had a pretty good run and that run is expected to continue. The broker is saying that if the shares take a dip, take advantage of this to buy in a bit cheaper. By purchasing shares when they are a bit cheaper you will be able to buy more of them than you would have if they were selling at a higher price. Should your investment view prove correct and the shares do perform well, you will be holding more of these well-performing assets.

Effective diversification

Diversification means not putting all your eggs in one basket. The way to do this is to spread your risk across asset classes and within each asset class. By doing this, if one element of the portfolio is doing poorly, some other investment may be stable or doing well and therefore should offset the adverse impact of the poorly performing investment.

Importantly, proper diversification doesn't simply serve to have the gain on one investment compensate for the loss on another. Effective diversification should also see the combined total of all investments advance in value. Having an investment strategy can help investors to be systematic in their diversification—rather than randomly picking different investments.

A diversified approach does not attempt to have small amounts invested in many different pies—this is ineffective diversification, and when transaction costs are included it can be counterproductive. The better approach is to have larger amounts in a few, carefully selected pies. This is diversifying with a strategy.

Understanding correlation

Correlation is the degree to which the movements of two different elements are related. A low correlation means that only a small or minor relationship is observable in the movement of the two elements. A high correlation means that there is a strong relationship between the two. For example, if every time one stock moved up in price by $1 another stock also moved up by a similar amount, we could say that those stocks are highly positively correlated. They tend to move in the same direction at the same times.

Figure 3.1 (see p. 30) compares BHP Billiton and Rio Tinto daily prices. These two stocks are highly correlated due to their earnings being affected by largely the same factors. Figure 3.2 (see p. 30) compares the materials sector with the health-care sector—this time we have two sectors with low correlation. Diversification is more effective when investments have lower correlation. Be cautious, however, before accepting the idea that low correlation is more important than smart share selection. It is very easy to be carried away with the study of correlation coefficients and build complex portfolios based around the interrelationships between the individual elements of that portfolio. The pursuit of low overall volatility may lead to mediocre results. You don't want to purchase a bad investment simply because the share price tends to move down when the others are moving up. If all your investments are moving up, that is a good thing. Furthermore, you must remember that correlation analysis is based on historical price action and there is no guarantee that these relationships will continue. Always apply logic first and then ask if the additional element adds any real value to your existing portfolio.

Compounding

Compounding is a process whereby the value of an investment or series of investments increases exponentially over time through profits from the investment being reinvested and so attracting more growth and profits.

In chapter 13 we will explore the various techniques investors can use to attempt to outperform the market index and predict potential movements in share prices. For now, however, it is essential you understand that investing in the sharemarket is generally a long-term activity.

Consistency and discipline

Failing to act in a disciplined and rigorous way — and doing so consistently over time — may result in poor performance. Consistency and discipline are important keys to financial market success.

As James O'Shaughnessy wrote in the investment classic *What Works on Wall Street*:

> Finding exploitable investment opportunities does not mean it's easy to make money. To do so requires the ability to consistently, patiently and slavishly stick with a strategy, even when it's performing poorly relative to other methods. Few are capable of such action.

Before we elaborate on consistency and discipline as the two keys to market success, we need to understand the market itself.

The efficient market hypothesis

The efficient market theory is used by some people to explain why many individual and professional investors fail to beat the market. It claims that there is no possibility, except by chance, that any person or group can outperform the market, and certainly no chance that the same person or group could consistently do so. But the problem with the efficient market hypothesis is that it assumes all investors act rationally and that all information is processed correctly—that is, that no-one makes mistakes.

Share traders do not always act rationally. During major market corrections—or worse, market crashes—fear takes over and people sell at prices they previously would not have accepted because they fear prices will fall further. And when people are desperate to get into a booming market they will pay much higher prices than the valuations put on those stocks in less bullish times. So even though a company's fundamentals may not have changed much, the psychology of the market has caused valuations to change. Another thing to consider is that investors do not necessarily process information the same way or at the same time. For example, an announcement that is positive for a company may see its price quickly pushed higher by early buyers. Later, other traders may only just be hearing the news. If they act on that information, it may provide nothing more than an opportunity for the early buyers to sell. You will also hear that a company's price recovered because it was oversold after investors overreacted to some bad news.

Given these examples, it is reasonable to assume that the efficient market does not always prevail and there are opportunities for investors to 'beat the market' by exploiting situations where they think shares are overpriced or underpriced.

Having said that, it is hard to do this on a sustained basis and investors who track the index will argue they are better off sticking to the index.

Be consistent

Sticking to a strategy just for the sake of it may not necessarily be the best thing if the strategy was flawed from the outset. I could have a strategy to only invest in loss-making companies. It is a strategy, but it is probably a bad one and sticking with it over the longer term is not going to make it any better. But if you have developed a strategy that is based on proper research that is cogent and perhaps has had the benefit of being reviewed by trusted advisers, it should be given time to deliver.

The biggest and best names in the sharemarket, and some of the wealthiest individuals in the world, are experts at being consistent. Warren Buffett and Peter Lynch are two world-famous fund managers who have developed their own models for share selection. They have very clear principles guiding what they will invest in and what companies they will not invest in. Their discipline and consistency of approach have at times caused them to underperform, but over the long term they have performed well.

At the height of the technology boom in 1999, Buffett's Berkshire Hathaway was targeted by the financial media and the financial press for failing to take advantage of the astronomical prices being paid for technology stocks. US companies were trading at up to 500 times earnings per share. In 1999, 279 internet companies listed in the United States and their average first-day gain was 90 per cent. At the time, the media, the analysts and investors were lured into believing that the bubble would never burst.

Market commentators pronounced 'this time is different' and 'this is a new era'. Buffett was told that he should retire, that he didn't understand the 'new economy' and that the 0.5 per cent return on his fund in 1999 was confirmation that his strategies no longer worked.

Buffett's strategy did not allow him to invest in internet or tech stocks so Berkshire Hathaway did not enjoy the exponential returns technology stocks were providing to more aggressive growth managers—at one point shares in his Berkshire Hathaway fund were down 30 per cent from US $65 000 per share to less than US $45 000 per share.

Despite the ongoing talk of 'the end of the old world economy' further reinforcing the idea that old economy company shares were dead and high-tech shares were the way of the future, Warren Buffett did not change his strategy.

In April 2000, when the NASDAQ took its first dive and the subsequent sell-off was labelled 'the tech wreck' by the media, the spotlight turned back to Buffett. The Berkshire Hathaway share price began to recover strongly and Buffett was asked to explain how he did it and what his secret was.

His answer was that there is no secret. All he did was act consistently. It is difficult to stick to a plan that is apparently not working. It is even more difficult when the world's financial media is telling you that you are wrong.

A plan should have financial targets in place to tell you when to reduce your activity or reassess your plan. Until those targets are met, it is generally beneficial to stick to the plan.

Following any methodology consistently means that you are likely to go through periods of poor performance, or what is referred to as 'drawdown'. It is extremely difficult to continue employing a method that is not working well—particularly when someone you know is enjoying a solid period of growth at the same time. Most people will be tempted to change their method or switch to a new method entirely. Provided you have thoroughly researched your technique, you should be aware of previous periods where the technique did not perform exceptionally well. What you are experiencing now may simply be normal in terms of the strategy's behaviour.

Drawdown

Drawdown is the period during which the equity in your account is falling because you have entered a period of losses.

A lack of consistency may result in underperformance. Following the recommendations of newsletters or of television personalities or magazines may be effective. However, the only way to determine whether those methods are effective is to follow them rigorously. And perhaps that is the most important advantage of a consistent approach: the ability to objectively assess whether a tipster, newsletter or television host is actually any good.

Having a strategy that is applied consistently may help free an investor from the emotions involved in the investing process.

Be patient

Part of a disciplined approach, and an important aspect in investing and trading, is patience. It may take time for the market to recognise what you may already have realised about a company's shares. It may take time for the company to generate profits and pay those out to shareholders. So if it takes time for all these good things to happen, why is it that we find it hard to wait for the time to pass?

A lack of patience is one culprit and fear is the other. Some investors may lack the patience to ride out the storm when investments are not performing as expected and they fear that things may never improve. Both are emotional responses. For many investors, selling out will be justified by explaining that the shares will be repurchased at a lower price. More likely, the investor will wait until things improve and the improvement is confirmed in the press. By this stage, any good news is already 'priced in'.

Even in short-term trading, patience is important to success. Traders must feel comfortable about allowing prices to trend long enough for an acceptable profit to accrue. During a period or string of losing trades, traders must be patient and continue to follow their plan through to the next winning trade.

Once a strategy has been researched, adopted and implemented, a healthy dollop of patience may help you to be more successful. However, before you decide to trade (or not to trade), you should carefully assess your experience, objectives and financial situation—and discuss your particular circumstances with your broker or professional adviser.

Further benefits of having a strategy for your share trading are discussed in the next chapter.

Appropriate asset allocation

Once you have determined your risk profile, current financial position, investment objectives, time frame and liquidity requirements, you need to work out what proportion of your total capital you want to invest in shares, property, fixed interest and cash. This is called 'asset allocation'.

Your risk/reward profile

Every investor has a different risk/reward profile. Taking the time to identify your own risk/reward profile will help you and your adviser choose the best investments for your needs. The three most common types are outlined below.

The cautious investor

Cautious investors seek better than basic returns, but insist that the risk must still be low. Typically older investors, they seek to protect wealth that they have accumulated. They may be prepared to consider growth investments that are less aggressive.

The prudent investor

Prudent investors want a balanced portfolio to work towards medium- to long-term financial goals. They require an investment strategy that will cope with the effects of tax and inflation. Calculated risks aimed at achieving greater returns, in the form of both income and growth, are acceptable to them.

The aggressive investor

Aggressive investors are prepared to take greater risks in pursuit of potentially higher long-term and short-term gains. They may take on a higher level of gearing and business risk.

Aggressive investors tend to view risk as an opportunity rather than a threat. They are driven by the potential for capital gain. Most of them are prepared to borrow money to invest. In terms of composition, their portfolios are very growth oriented.

*   *   *

You are unlikely to get very far along your investment journey without encountering the term 'fundamental analysis'. Looking at a particular company, its competitors and its sector, as well as the economic climate, are all part of this type of analysis. There are some key financial ratios used in fundamental analysis and chapter 13 introduces these.

Fundamental analysis

So far, we have discussed some of the mechanics of buying and selling shares, and covered some of the reasons for developing an investment strategy when creating a diversified portfolio. For those investors who like to undertake their own analysis or want a better understanding of how their adviser may make an individual share recommendation, this chapter and the next one will introduce two broad approaches to share analysis: fundamental analysis and technical analysis.

Fundamental analysis is the study of the various factors that affect a company's earnings and dividends, as well as the impact on the relative safety of an investment in a certain company due to the relationship between its share price and the various elements of its financial position and performance.

Fundamental analysis also involves a detailed examination of the company's competitors, the industry or sector it is within, and perhaps the domestic and global economic climate. Fundamental analysts may examine the growth prospects for the sector. Future levels of general economic activity are also used to help determine whether a company's prospects are improving or not.

Fundamental analysis can be quantitative, which involves looking at the hard numbers and either developing benchmarks or hurdles for the individual company to exceed or ranking companies by the resultant ratios. Fundamental analysis can also be qualitative. Qualitative analysis is more subjective—for example, it may be a discussion with the directors of the company about their growth prospects or it could be a conversation with that company's customers or competitors.

Fundamental analysis is forward-looking even though the data used is by and large historical. This raises an important limitation of fundamental analysis, as we will see.

Intrinsic value

Intrinsic value is the actual value or book price of a security, as opposed to its current market value. The measurement of intrinsic value is subjective because it depends on the valuation method employed.

Fundamental analysis is used to determine what the company should be worth, its 'intrinsic value', and/or its growth prospects. This intrinsic value can then be compared to the current value of the company as measured by the share price and market capitalisation. If the shares are trading at less than the intrinsic value, they may be seen as good value or as offering a cheap 'entry' price. If, however, the intrinsic value calculated by the fundamental analyst is lower than the current share price, the analyst may place a sell recommendation on the shares or, at best, a hold recommendation.

It is essential to gain a sound understanding of how to value shares and measure the efficiency and profitability of a business and its management.

One aspect of fundamental analysis that we will be examining more closely is ratio analysis and the importance of some of the many ratios. We will also look at the limitations of this analysis.

What are you trying to learn about the company?

Share investors must be clear about what knowledge they are seeking. There are some basic principles that should be remembered and questions that should be asked. When you are about to review the financials, current and historical, keep these points in the back of your mind:

¤ Historical costs give a poor approximation of real values.

¤ Don't draw conclusions from a single financial item in isolation.

¤ Companies are multidimensional. For example, debt funding may have increased dramatically. While this may initially be perceived as a negative if there are no sales to help generate cash to pay the interest, it could be a positive if used correctly. Indeed, not enough debt can also be viewed as sub-optimal.

¤ Check where the projected growth is going to come from.

¤ Consolidated statements could be hiding poor results in a particular sector of the group.

When you start drilling into the detail, ask yourself:

¤ *Is the growth in turnover being achieved organically or through acquisition?* (If acquired, will turnover remain the same once fully integrated into the company?)

¤ *To what extent do current profits reflect one-off events?*

¤ *Will the profits and growth rates be sustainable over the longer term?* This depends on industry structural issues (how many competitors) as well as the economy. What is the company's pricing power? Are there natural barriers to entry that may prevent a competitor from entering and reducing prices?

In fundamental analysis, in-depth research into a company is compiled. Several statements are examined. These include the company's:

¤ balance sheet

¤ profit and loss statement

¤ cash flow statement

¤ letter to shareholders.

Value investing

We will now look at an example of a fundamental-analysis approach that attempts to rank companies according to whether they represent good 'value'. This is an example of a possible strategy only and you should obtain advice from a professional adviser prior to making any investment decisions.

Value-based investing is a style where investments are only held as long as they represent good value. The approach can be applied at each stage of the investing process. Even top-down managers, who begin the investment selection process by looking at countries, markets and sectors before looking at the individual company, may determine that country A represents better value than country B; that industry A represents better value than industry B; and, finally, that company A represents better value than company B. For both top-down managers and bottom-up managers, who start by investigating individual companies, selection is usually based on certain value criteria such as price to earnings, dividend yield, price to cash flow and price to net tangible assets.

Value investing is essentially contrarian in nature. We know that from time to time markets can misprice companies. This mispricing is often the result of emotions—when emotions are extremely enthusiastic or depressed, prices for companies do not accurately reflect the long-term fundamentals of the company. When the majority of investors do not favour particular companies despite 'good fundamentals', these stocks can become 'good value'. There is a large number of value managers in Australia, including those regarded as deep value managers. The philosophy of deep value managers is quite simple and this in turn makes adherence to the proposed strategy easier. Deep value managers look for shares that are out of favour with the market but which are predicted to regain favour once the market recognises their 'true value'.

The investment process

The investment process for value investing starts by confining the share 'universe' to a certain number of the largest and most liquid Australian shares that are trading in the most volume, as these are the most readily tradable shares. The shares are then compared on a like-for-like basis, looking at measures such as projected balance sheets, profit and loss and cash flows, and valuing the forecast earnings. The managers then forecast a value for the shares at a specified time in the future, calculate the expected investment returns and then rank all the shares on a daily basis.

Filters are then applied to select a certain number of shares. This number varies depending on the strategy of the manager.

From the strategies of value managers, a process of share selection that is simple and that lends itself well to emulation can be developed. An example is set out below. This technique is something that an investor may use as a starting point to determine its suitability:

1   Select the most frequently traded 100 companies from the S&P/ASX 200, using trading volume figures.

2   Determine a three-year forecast of intrinsic 'fair value' based on P/E ratio, EPS growth and dividends using historical data.

3   Rank shares according to best relative value.

4   Select the top 25 to 35 for the portfolio.

5   Monitor the investments regularly to ensure they continue to meet requirements and standards.

6   Sell off investments that no longer meet the criteria.

A simpler approach

An example of a simpler approach to value investing is the Australian version of the 'Dogs of the Dow' strategy, originally developed by Michael O'Higgins in the United States.

The steps are:

1   Start with the top 50 industrial companies by market capitalisation.

2   Rank them in descending order by dividend yield.

3   Buy equal dollar amounts of the top-10 ranked companies.

4   Hold for one or two years and repeat the process.

Before you conduct any investment activity, you should speak with your financial adviser and determine the suitability of this strategy to your needs.

Market ratios

Some investors live and breathe market ratios. All their assessments are based on the numbers. Others take a more qualitative view to assessing companies and others again use a mixture of both.

When dealing with ratios there is no avoiding the numbers! But you do not need to memorise how all these ratios are calculated here and now. However, the further you travel on your investment journey and the more you read analysts' reports and the financial press, the more familiar these ratios will become to you. So even if you do not study this section now, it would be advisable to read it so that you know what's available. Then, perhaps you can revisit this section at a later time when you need to.

A step towards successful investing is to relate a company's performance to the price of its shares. By calculating 'per share' data we can compare earnings, corporate health and even debt to a company's share price.

How earnings affect share prices

In his model for reflexivity, one of the world's most infamous speculators, George Soros, explains that a strong driver of share price is a company's earnings. As earnings rise and are retained by the company, the value of the shares to the shareholder rises and so the price of the shares also rises as investors, keen to gain access to the higher earnings, become increasingly willing to pay the higher prices.

Soros's model is shown in figure 13.1. In the model, it is evident that as the earnings rise, the share price also rises. Just as the share price starts to rise, however, you will notice some divergence. See how the share price is falling even though the earnings are still rising? What is happening here? Has the market got it wrong? On the contrary—the market is looking ahead. The market believes the high share price has factored in or taken into account the very best the company could produce and the market is now looking ahead. The market perhaps expects future declines in earnings and sell-offs in anticipation of this future decline. Investors who have held the share for some time perhaps believe this is all they are going to get, and taking profits becomes an important objective.

Figure 13.1: Soros's model of reflexivity

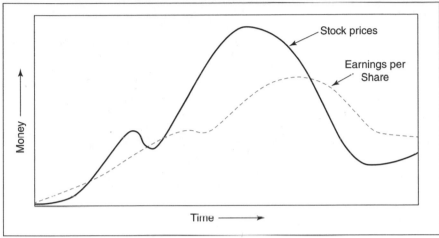

Source: *Alchemy of Finance* by George Soros © 1994 by George Soros. Reprinted with permission of John Wiley & Sons, Inc.

However, when earnings continue to rise, more buyers enter the market and more favourable reports are published in the media. This enthusiasm pushes the share price above earnings per share. With time, however, the over-optimistic bias is recognised as such and expectations lower, causing prices to plummet to a point below earnings. The underlying earnings trend reverses, which reinforces the drop in prices. Finally, the pessimism of the market stabilises and the cycle moves back to its starting point.

With that understanding of how supply, demand and expectations regarding earnings affect share prices, we will now look at a number of important market ratios.

Earnings per share

The earnings per share (EPS) of a company are found using the formula below.

$$EPS = \frac{\text{Net profit after tax (NPAT)}}{\text{Number of shares on issue}} = \text{Cents per share}$$

An EPS figure on its own means very little. It could include non-recurring items, so it is important that the analyst looks at net profit *after* tax but *before* any of the non-recurring items referred to as 'abnormal items'. Further, the company may not necessarily pay this amount out as a dividend.

For the successful share investor, it is important to check whether the EPS has been rising or at least has been relatively stable. While this requirement will be dependent on the strategy selected, the criterion of a stable or rising earnings stream over many years may help to prevent investment in companies that are later liquidated and delisted at a loss to the investor.

From the formula, it is easy to see that there are only two ways EPS can fall—either profits decline or the number of shares increases. For the active investor, too much of either is not a good thing. A lower profit means the investor earns less, and a larger number of shareholders to share the profit with also means lower profits.

After determining the current EPS, look for trends. Has EPS been growing or falling, and how much profit is from operations rather than one-off events? If EPS is the same as last year, has there been an increase in the shares on issue? Remember—EPS does not lend itself to the determination of 'quality'. In bear markets, analysts look much more closely at the quality of earnings and quickly dismiss one-off items. During good times, analysis may be a little more relaxed and less conservative.

Price/earnings ratio

The price/earnings ratio (P/E ratio) shows how many times, in years, it will take for your purchase to be covered by earnings. It is determined by using the formula below.

$$P/E \text{ ratio} = \frac{\text{Share price}}{\text{EPS}} = \text{Times covered by earnings}$$

This is one of the easiest ratios to use. The P/E ratio provides an immediate comparison tool. Investors must realise, however, that P/E ratios are often based on historical earnings and therefore may be of little real use in determining a share's value. It may be more important and more useful to use prospective earnings in the P/E ratio calculation.

The P/E ratio reflects the market's view of the earnings potential of the company.

A low P/E ratio compared to the average P/E of the sector that the company belongs to could indicate one of three things:

¤ The share is underpriced.

¤ The share is correctly priced due to the quality (or lack thereof) of the earnings.

¤ The share is overpriced because the entire sector has become fashionable and the earnings are unsustainable.

Some P/Es have been shown to be based more on faith (or hype) than on substance, but solidly performing growth-oriented companies tend to have consistently higher P/E ratios. On its own, however, the P/E ratio does not really say very much. It is much more effective when used in conjunction with other measures, such as return on equity, which is discussed later in this chapter.

Dividend per share

Dividend per share (DPS) is simply the earnings payout received in your hand in cents per share, as shown below.

$$DPS = \frac{\text{Total dividend paid}}{\text{Number of shares on issue}} = \text{Cents per share}$$

A thorough analyst does not merely observe consistent dividend payment over many years and then determine the investment to be 'safe' or the company a 'blue chip'. It is essential to check whether the dividends were paid from the current year's earnings or from retained earnings of previous years.

To do that, you can check the payout ratio or dividends/earnings, which shows what percentage of earnings was paid out as a dividend. The reciprocal is earnings/dividends, which is the dividend cover ratio. If the dividend cover ratio is less than one, the dividends must have been paid out of retained earnings.

Sometimes paying out all the earnings as dividends is not a good thing — for example, perhaps an above-average rate of return could be gained from using the money to fund expansion or an acquisition instead of paying dividends. At other times, if the company cannot do anything with the earnings, it will pay out a special dividend or announce a return of capital. For shareholders in good-quality companies, it may be an advantage for the company and the remaining shareholders if funds were used in a share buyback.

Dividend yield

The dividend yield is the dividend expressed as a percentage of the share price, as shown in the formula below.

$$\text{Dividend yield} = \frac{\text{Dividends per share}}{\text{Share price}} \times 100 = \%$$

This is the rate that can be used to compare the income generated from one investment to that from another. Later we will see that, due to the benefits of franking, a dividend yield of 5 per cent may be more beneficial than earning interest of 5 per cent.

High dividend yields are attractive, but even if a company is showing a dividend yield of 11 per cent and every other company in the same sector is showing a dividend yield of 5 per cent, it may not mean that the company under investigation is going to pay a high dividend. The above formula for determining the dividend yield shows there are two components that determine the yield — last year's dividend and the current price. A high dividend yield may have been driven by a lower share price, and, given that the dividend yield is based on last year's dividend, the lower price may indicate that the market expects next year's dividend to be lower. Nevertheless, as we will see later, market participants regularly panic, driving prices down in expectation of significantly lower dividends, only to find later that their pessimism was unfounded.

Dividend cover ratio

The dividend cover ratio is how many times current earnings cover the dividend paid.

Cash flow per share

The formula for cash flow per share is shown below.

$$\text{Cash flow per share} = \frac{\text{NPAT} + \text{Depreciation}}{\text{Number of shares on issue}} = \text{Cents per share}$$

In the formula to determine cash flow per share, you will note that most analysts add back the depreciation because it is a non-cash expense. By adding back the depreciation (and other non-cash expenses), we arrive at a proxy for the cash earnings of the business.

Cash is an extremely important part of evaluating a company, and it becomes even more important when the economy slows and company earnings are being examined with more scrutiny. The 'cash is king' adage is rarely considered during periods of boom when momentum investing and growth strategies take the fore. At the first hint of slowing growth or the first mention of the word 'recession' professionals in the market begin touting the benefits of defensive strategies.

'Defensive' can mean a number of things—it can mean finding companies with earnings that are shielded from the slowing economy or ones that are derived predominantly from a country that is not subject to the slowdown. It can also mean finding companies with either a large proportion of their earnings in cash or large cash reserves. Companies with large amounts of cash or cash earnings are considered good options with defensive strategies because they are able to weather the storm and continue to pay out cash dividends or pay down some of their debt. For these reasons, focusing on cash may be a worthwhile endeavour.

Capital ratios

Capital ratios measure management's efficiency in the use of a company's capital and are an important indicator of a company's long-term stability. The most important capital ratios for our purposes are the debt-to-equity ratios, which indicate the company's level of gearing. The formulas for these ratios are shown in these equations.

$$\text{Debt-to-equity ratio} = \frac{\text{Total borrowings}}{\text{Shareholder's equity}} \times 100 = \%$$

$$\text{Net debt-to-equity ratio} = \frac{\text{Total borrowings} - \text{cash}}{\text{Shareholder's equity}} \times 100 = \%$$

There are principally two sources of funding for a company—debt and equity. The question for the company is, 'What is the right mix?' A company with a high proportion of debt is said to be highly leveraged or geared. Should the entity borrow more money or raise capital through the issue of shares? Doctorates have been devoted, and chairs endowed, to the pursuit of finding the right mix. Measures such as the weighted average cost of capital have been devised, and many academics and investors swear by this and the other various models that have been developed to determine both the correct mix and which source of funding to use for a given project.

Generally, debt is regarded as a cheaper source of funds than equity and so the higher the debt levels the better the return on the equity. Too high a debt level, though, and the margin of safety for a company begins to erode, so while it is important that debt is used, the company should not overextend itself. Nevertheless, if equity levels are too high compared to debt, the return to shareholders will be lower.

There are other disadvantages of too much debt. Credit ratings can be compromised and the cost of funding the debt can rise if interest rates increase. During times of low interest rates, this is often not a concern; however, if interest rates rise the cost of funding the debt could become onerous. For these reasons it is important that management strikes an appropriate balance.

To assess the correct level we need to ask 'what if' questions—for example, how would cash flows be affected if a recession were to transpire or if interest rates went up?

Profitability ratios

Profitability ratios are the basic test of a company's profit performance. Three important profitability ratios are return on equity, return on assets and profit margin, as shown in these equations.

$$\text{Return on equity} = \frac{\text{NPAT}}{\text{Shareholder's equity}} \times 100 = \%$$

$$\text{Return on assets} = \frac{\text{Earnings before interest and tax (EBIT)}}{\text{Total assets}} \times 100 = \%$$

$$\text{Profit margin} = \frac{\text{NPAT}}{\text{Sales revenue}} \times 100 = \%$$

Profitability ratios measure a company's ability to earn solid, high, sustainable and/or non-volatile profits. They measure the return the company is making on funds or other resources it has at its disposal. The return generated here, however, is not the same as that which the shareholders receive, as not all the earnings generated are paid out as dividends. Indeed, sometimes no dividends are paid out at all and the profits are reinvested by the company.

The numbers generated by these profitability ratios reflect how clever the company has been in earning money on the funds invested by the shareholders. The ability of a company to earn a decent return means it can attract future funding, perhaps at more desirable rates, and management may also gain favour with the investment community.

The results are generally an indication of a company's financial wellbeing. The greater the amount of money that a company can generate, the more it can grow, and, as we mentioned earlier, it is growth that is necessary for sustained price increases.

Importantly, investors should remember that profitability is different from absolute profits. Profitability is the rate of return over some other part of the business—such as what the investors have entrusted to management (equity), the total resources at management's disposal (assets) or the sales that the company generates.

As a shareholder you are an owner, and as such it is you who takes on the risk of whether a company can earn a sustainable profit over a number of years. The value of the shares you hold depends firstly on the profit-making record of the entity. So these numbers produce some of the most important indications of the quality of the business you own or are considering owning a part of.

Also worth mentioning is that it is through these ratios that most of the adjustments are made and numbers are tinkered with by analysts. For example:

¤ Extraordinary and/or abnormal items can be taken out to better reflect true recurring after-tax profits, meaning the figure used is often net profit after tax but before abnormal items.

¤ Share issues and various classes of shares (such as bonus issues and rights issues, and company options) are adjusted for, to more accurately reflect the return to ordinary shareholders. The profit figures given after these adjustments are called 'fully diluted earnings'.

Liquidity ratios

Liquidity ratios show a company's ability to pay its short-term debt and the amount that shareholders would receive should the company be liquidated. Three important liquidity ratios are the current ratio, the quick ratio and net tangible asset (NTA) backing. The formulas for these are shown in these equations.

$$\text{Current ratio} = \frac{\text{Current assets}}{\text{Current liabilities}} = \text{Times covered}$$

$$\text{Quick ratio} = \frac{\text{Current assets} - \text{Inventories}}{\text{Current liabilities}} = \text{Times covered}$$

$$\text{NTA backing} = \frac{\text{Shareholder's equity} - \text{Intangibles}}{\text{Number of shares on issue}} = \text{Cents per share}$$

Appropriate numbers for the liquidity ratios are crucial to the survival of a business, particularly during times of adversity. If short-term assets are less than short-term liabilities the company may be insolvent, and under corporations law operating while insolvent is an offence. Failure to pay down debts on time can also hurt a company's credit ratings and future cost of funds, and even threaten its existence.

The current ratio is also known as the working capital ratio. It measures the excess of current assets over current liabilities and so, in turn, it measures short-term liquidity of the company and its ability to meet short-term debt obligations.

The general rule of thumb for a current ratio is 2 to 1—that is, $2 of current assets for every $1 of current liabilities. Importantly, this general rule will not change, regardless of the strategy employed.

Each industry's activity cycle, however, has a different length. The activity cycle is the time that elapses between money being paid out for the purchase of raw materials or goods and the revenue being received upon sale of the company's products. Longer activity cycles suggest a company will take longer to be paid, and this must be supported by a higher current ratio.

There are plenty of hurdles prior to the revenue-generation stage and receipt of funds. Processing of raw materials, construction, drying, shipping, importing and exporting are all steps in the activity cycle for various industries. If interest is owed in the short term, cash flow must be carefully managed and a buffer of current assets—particularly cash and its equivalents—must be available to meet payments when they fall due.

The quick ratio, or acid test ratio, is similar to the current ratio described above; however, the quick ratio removes inventory and looks at what assets can contribute to cash in the next month or two to help meet liabilities due for payment during that period. With the quick ratio we can assess what the implications for short-term debt facilitation may be if a company suffers slowing inventory sales.

Another ratio that falls under the liquidity banner is interest cover. Interest cover describes how many times the interest expense can be covered by the profits (before interest and tax) of the business. Generally, a higher ratio is better; however, it could also indicate that the company could expand with the use of leverage.

Use of fundamental ratio analysis

Before we move on from the topic of ratio analysis, it is perhaps worth remembering that, as with all analysis, there are limitations to the effectiveness of ratio analysis. Some of the difficulties arise because there is simply too much data, the data is imperfect, or it may have already been factored in by other market participants, rendering it somewhat less than useful for a timely signal to act. Perhaps it will make matters clearer if we say that fundamentals may help to determine what, not when, to buy.

Having an understanding of fundamental ratios is essential to successful long-term investing. For example, there is a high correlation between changes in a company's earnings over more than 10 years and that company's share price. Understanding the ratios alone, however, is not sufficient for investment success. The successful share trader must be able to demonstrate a method of utilising the information provided by the ratios in a logical, consistent and disciplined manner.

The strategies we discuss in this book are all focused on finding long-term investment opportunities. As such, the strategies may be subject to the short-term volatility of the market. The strategies you develop may fall under several categories — growth, value, contrarian or momentum, or a hybrid of some description. Indeed, for the purposes of diversification it may make perfect sense to run several strategies simultaneously.

A strategy is simply a set of carefully researched and selected rules, established by the individual investor, regarding which ratios to use, how to combine them and when to use them. The rules, however, form only part of the strategy. The investor will also require rules that cover when to sell (if at all), how to weight the portfolio, how to re-weight the portfolio and when and how to add to the portfolio. Every contingency must be covered.

What should you do if one of the companies you purchased is the target of a takeover? Will you automatically accept the first bid? What will you do with the funds? What will you do with income received from dividends? Will you hold those dividends in cash until some future re-weighting date or will you automatically reinvest? All of these questions require an answer or your strategy can't be described as 'carefully planned'.

* * *

Few investors would make decisions to buy or sell without looking at the share price chart of a company's performance. A common view is that fundamental analysis assists in the decision of what to buy or sell and technical analysis helps to decide when. Chapter 14 explains technical analysis and the most frequently used charts.

Technical analysis

Technical analysis is the study of the past price movements of an individual share, a market sector or the market as a whole to gain an insight into where the price might go.

Charts convert a table of data into an easy-to-interpret graph. Take the example of figure 14.1 (overleaf): is it easier to tell the share's recent price history by looking at the table or the graph? The graph provides a quick snapshot of how the company's share price has travelled.

Figure 14.1: table of data versus line graph

Date	Opening	High	Low	Close
Day 1	13.86	13.97	13.84	13.87
Day 2	13.82	13.91	13.78	13.91
Day 3	13.85	13.90	13.80	13.84
Day 4	13.82	13.84	13.66	13.71
Day 5	13.60	13.81	13.46	13.65
Day 6	13.58	13.74	13.53	13.70
Day 7	13.85	14.13	13.85	13.90
Day 8	13.90	14.12	13.88	14.00
Day 9	14.20	14.40	14.11	14.40
Day 10	14.39	14.63	14.25	14.44
Day 11	14.62	14.80	14.52	14.62
Day 12	14.55	14.58	14.41	14.52
Day 13	14.57	14.64	14.22	14.37
Day 14	14.32	14.40	14.15	14.20
Day 15	14.30	14.77	14.30	14.61

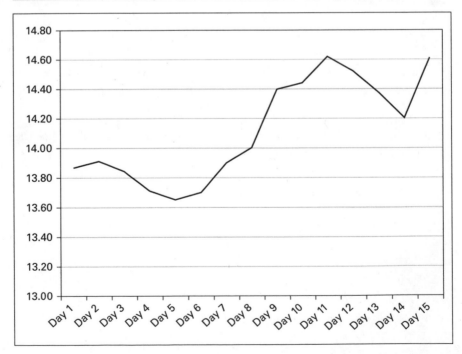

To understand where technical analysis fits in, let's examine the objectives of both fundamental and technical analysis. Notwithstanding whether investors are aiming for income or capital growth, the main objective is clearly to make money from rising share prices. According to fundamental analysis, economists and market strategists make observations and forecasts about such things as new car registrations, new home sales, retail sales, unemployment, gross domestic product and inflation in an effort to determine whether or not the economy is growing or slowing.

Technical analysts argue we can study all of the economic factors, and incorporate the theory from all of the experts, and come up with a view on whether the sharemarket is going to go up or down, or we can simply look at the share prices themselves, which reflect the collective influence of all of the above factors.

The argument in support of technical analysis is that all buying, selling, rumours and statistics will be factored into the price of a share as people act on that information. By looking at the prices we can see whether there is buying, which would result in rising prices. We know if bad news has come out, or if it is expected to be released, because sellers come into the market and push prices lower. Proponents of charting and technical analysis suggest that we can obtain all of the information we need by observing the prices and we do not need to look at anything else.

Anyone can use charts

We can look at a chart and draw some simple conclusions. Take a look at the chart in figure 14.2 (overleaf). We can see without knowing anything about the company and without even knowing the company name that the share price peaked in February. There may have been a lot of good news coming out or just one factor. Technical analysts suggest that there are methods we can use to determine simply if the share price is in an upward or downward movement. Therefore, we do not need to worry so much about what news is being released. Charts, according to technical analysts, reflect all the available information at any given time. If someone has information that no-one else has and they act upon that information, they will affect the price and it will move to a new level.

Figure 14.2: an example of a sharemarket chart

Forget the idea that charts can predict the future. They can't, and neither can fundamental analysis. We can, however, use some simple charting techniques that may assist in the development of a worthwhile strategy by giving us an insight into the underlying sentiment in the market.

Before we look at developing some of our techniques, let's break technical analysis down into its various subcategories. You may elect to develop your own combination of the techniques that are available and discover something unique.

Technical analysis can be broken down into three categories:

¤ classic technical analysis

¤ indicators

¤ cycles in price and time—for example, Gann or Elliott Wave theory.

Classic technical analysis

We will discuss classic technical analysis and indicators in this chapter. However, price and time cycles are not discussed in this book.

In this section we will build a technique using three tools:

⌘ trends

⌘ resistance and support lines

⌘ chart patterns.

Trends

Various different charts are used to analyse price action—for example, line charts, point and figure charts, market profiles and candlesticks. However, the most common type of chart is the bar chart.

Bar charts

Bar charts have a single bar consisting of an open price, a high, a low and a close price for a particular period.

A bar chart simply takes the information from the day's trading and plots it, as shown in figure 14.3. On the right-hand side of figure 14.3 is a single day's 'bar'.

Figure 14.3: how to derive a single day's 'bar'

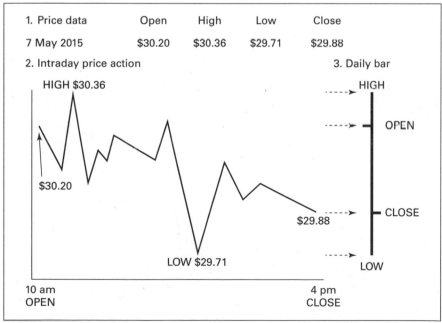

Bar charts plot price data as a vertical bar. A tab on the left side of the bar represents the open, and a tab on the right of the bar represents the close. By plotting each day consecutively on a chart the technical analyst develops a picture that helps to illustrate the interplay between supply (sellers) and demand (buyers). While we have drawn a daily bar, it is just as easy to draw a weekly chart by capturing the open on Monday, the highest high and the lowest low during the week, and finally the close on Friday afternoon. We can also construct monthly bar charts and even one-minute bar charts the same way.

Using bar charts

The first step for technical analysts is to define the 'trend'. A trend is a period when the price seems to be moving more in one direction than the other. Figures 14.4 and 14.5 illustrate clearly definable trends.

Figure 14.4: an example of a downtrend

Clearly it is in the interest of technical analysts to use their tools to select those shares that are exhibiting uptrends. An old adage familiar to traders is relevant at this point—'the trend is your friend'.

Figure 14.5: an example of an uptrend

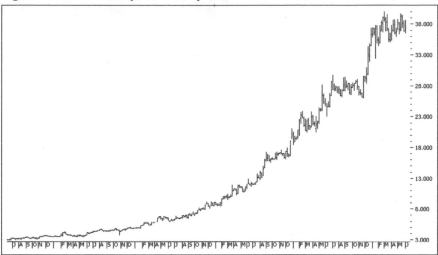

An uptrend is a trend in which the share is rising in price. This is a 'friendly' environment for owning shares. Assuming we are not using derivatives or short-selling techniques, we make capital gains from rising prices and thus are most interested in isolating these upward trends.

Defining a trend

Figure 14.6 (overleaf) illustrates how easy it is to define an uptrend. Its simplicity is a little embarrassing—but only because so many of us are guilty of buying shares that are not only not in uptrends but are actually in clearly definable downtrends! Notice that each subsequent high is higher than the previous high, while each subsequent low is also higher than the previous low. This is how an uptrend is defined.

Figure 14.6: a simple uptrend

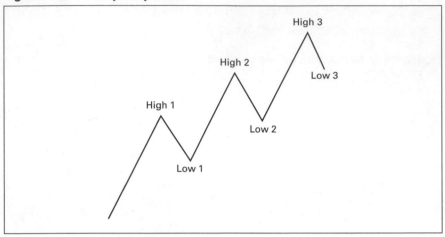

You must have higher highs and higher lows to have an uptrend. If you do not have both, you do not have an uptrend. However, you might not have a downtrend either.

Figure 14.7 shows a downtrend. The definition of a downtrend is lower lows and lower highs. If you look at figure 14.7, you can see that each high is lower than the previous one and each low is lower than the previous one. From a technical analyst's perspective you are doing yourself a disservice if you purchase shares that are in a downtrend. It is deemed prudent to wait until an uptrend emerges.

Figure 14.7: a simple downtrend

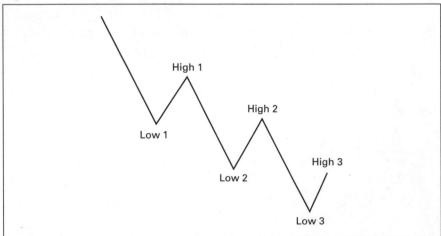

Markets, however, are not as simple as the diagrams, and there are periods when the market is in neither an uptrend nor a downtrend. Figure 14.8 helps illustrate this point.

Figure 14.8: neither an uptrend nor a downtrend

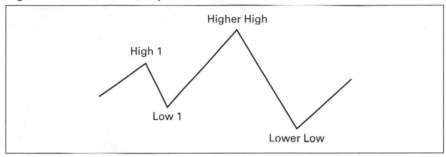

In figure 14.8 prices never reach a point where there is a succession of higher highs and a higher low. After the market registered the higher high, notice that the market then made a lower low. There is neither an uptrend nor a downtrend; the market is merely trading sideways with little indication of clear direction. This is known as 'range trading'. There are tools available that enable you to trade in a sideways-trending market, but these are not discussed in this book. For most investors, though, a sideways-trending market represents a time to stand aside and do nothing.

Recognising a change of trend

We have now defined an uptrend and a downtrend as well as a period of range trading or sideways movement. The next step is to make use of them in the marketplace. Obviously, we would like to get out of downtrends as soon as they develop and we would like to enter into uptrends as soon as they are confirmed. Now that we know what these trends are, it should be easier to locate them.

In figure 14.9 (overleaf), it is easy to see that initially there was an uptrend in place. There is a series of higher highs (H1 and H2) and a series of higher lows (L1, L2 and L3). Notice, however, that H3 is lower than the previous high. This is the first warning that the market is no longer in an uptrend, as the criteria for an uptrend are no longer being met. At point H3, there are still higher lows but there are also lower highs, and we need both to be higher for an uptrend to continue. At point H3, there is no trend either up or down. We may describe the market as neutral or range-bound.

Figure 14.9: identifying trends

The price in figure 14.9 then turns lower and breaks the level marked by L3. Indeed, if you look carefully, something significant has happened. There is a lower high at H3 and a lower low once L3 is breached. There is a lower high and a lower low. A downtrend is in place at the point marked D.

Establishing the direction of the market or share by determining whether it is in an uptrend, downtrend or sidewards trend can simplify the process of sorting through myriad shares and markets, enabling a search for the best opportunities. It should also save time as determining the trend is objective and requires little interpretation. You should not have to spend hours poring over charts trying to determine where the market is going. Defining the trend should take less than five minutes and can be done at a glance.

Resistance and support lines

While there are some limitations with classic technical analysis, it can provide some assistance in fine-tuning the timing of a change in trend. Let's look at using support and resistance levels to help define the buying and selling points in the market.

Resistance line

A resistance line is the level at which rising prices stop climbing and move sidewards or downwards, indicating an abundance of supply.

By drawing a line that connects all of the highs, we create what is called a resistance line. At this level, the market resists going higher because there are sellers who enter the market to sell more shares when the share trades at this price. The weight of their cumulative selling prevents the price from rising. Figure 14.10 shows resistance and support lines.

Figure 14.10: resistance and support lines

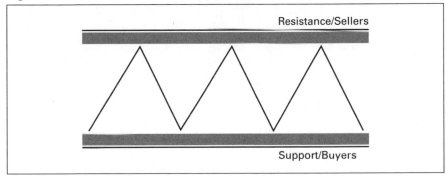

If the price were to break through this resistance, as it has in figure 14.11, it could suggest that sales at this price are complete or that the sellers have decided not to sell any more of the share for the time being. Either way, it could be supportive for the share and may even reflect the release of good news, which has resulted in sellers at the resistance price holding off or changing their minds. Technical analysts see a break of resistance as a buy signal.

Figure 14.11: break of resistance line

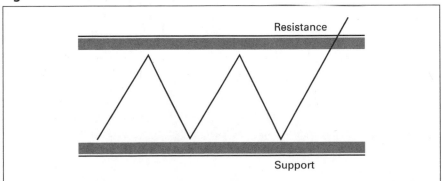

Support line

A support line is the level at which declining prices stop falling and move sideways or upwards because there is sufficient demand for the share to stop the price falling any further.

By drawing a line that connects the lows of the range we can show the level of support. The price is supported (stopped) from going lower by the presence of a buyer or buyers at this price. Each time the price drops to this support level, buying emerges that is of sufficient volume to absorb the selling and prevent the price from falling through.

Suppose the price does break through the support level, as shown in figure 14.12—what would this indicate? The first conclusion we may draw is that the buyers at the previous support price are no longer present (at that price at least). The buying has dried up and the selling is continuing now at lower prices. This selling at lower prices suggests that the sellers are becoming more aggressive.

Figure 14.12: break of support line

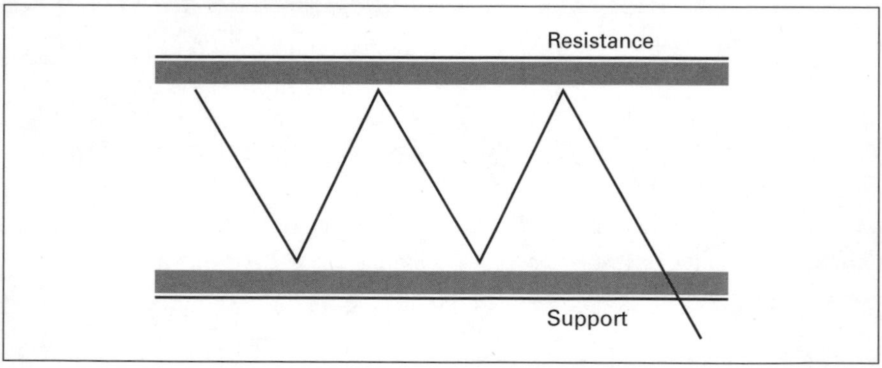

Volume

Volume is an important tool for technical analysts and we could fill many pages talking about volume in all its various guises. What is most important for you to know at this stage is that rising volume at the time of a break of support or resistance is generally regarded as further confirmation that the break is legitimate and that the price is expected to continue moving in the same direction. This could be for a number of reasons—for example, the higher volumes may suggest more sophisticated and knowledgeable investors are establishing positions in the direction of the market's move, or it could be simply because more individuals are discovering the particular factors that make an investment or trade in this share attractive. For technical analysts, finding reasons why this is the case is less important than what the chart is telling them—that the price is expected to continue to move in the same direction. Figure 14.13 shows how volume can be used in conjunction with breaks of support or resistance.

Figure 14.13: using volume with support and resistance lines

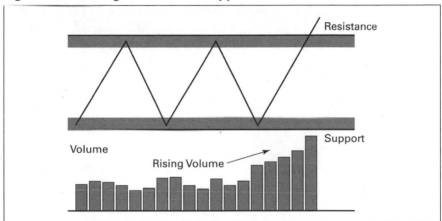

Chart patterns

There are many books available for the classic technical analyst. These books look at the variety of 'patterns' that the market prices form. These patterns are traded by classic technical analysts and, like all tools in trading and investing, do not work all the time. Figure 14.14 (overleaf) describes one pattern, known as a rising triangle. We will discuss this pattern further. However, there are many other patterns, and if you are interested in doing further research on this subject you should look into the various books available. In figure 14.14, you can see that the resistance line is flat.

Figure 14.14: a rising triangle chart pattern

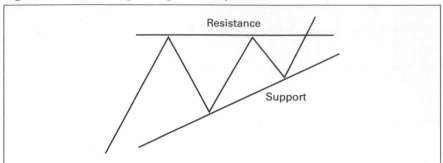

This suggests that there is enough selling to absorb the buying at the same price. The support level, however, is sloping upwards. This suggests that the buyers are becoming progressively more aggressive and are increasingly willing to pay higher prices. The question you might ask is why. As noted before, technical analysts do not concern themselves with the answer. By looking at the chart, we can see that the buyers are more aggressive and so the price could go higher. If the price breaks through that resistance level, the picture is as follows—buyers are more aggressive, paying higher prices, while the selling that was evident before dries up or ceases.

According to technical analysts, prices should go higher. If you add rising volume to the picture, you have another validation of the strength being exhibited in the market. A cautionary reminder is worth mentioning at this point—nothing works all the time. The typical trader might buy the share as it rises through resistance. We are, however, unaware of what the future holds. Therefore, despite the aggressive buyers, the selling drying up and the rising volume, we may buy the share only to see it simply drop back in price. This may happen to traders many times before they get it right.

'Let your profits run and cut your losses' is a piece of investing advice that has stood the test of time. It is better for a trader to take a small loss quickly than to watch the price deteriorate even further and incur a bigger loss later. Successful traders may get it wrong many more times than they get it right but, because the losses are kept small, the fewer but much larger winning trades should outweigh the collective losses.

Successful traders still have losing trades—they may have many losing trades—but what makes them successful is that they are able to recover quickly from those losing trades.

The next step

While the classic technical analysis described above does help identify potential share opportunities, it is essential that you develop an objective process before jumping in and risking your money. A possible process is illustrated in figure 14.15. First, define those shares that are in uptrends. If they are not in an uptrend, put them aside. Do not try to imagine your favourite share being in an uptrend that does not exist. The next step is to apply a filter to confirm the trend and provide a further prerequisite. Once these requirements are met, we can apply entry and exit methods to trigger the purchase or sale of the share.

Figure 14.15: the process of share selection

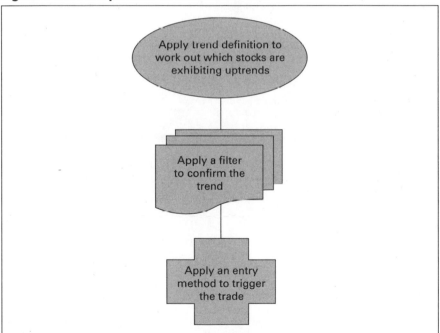

Adding a filter

There are many filters or indicators available to apply to shares, and many people get carried away. A filter or indicator is a proviso added to a set of conditions allowing, or disallowing, certain actions to be taken.

Two common mistakes are made at this step. The first is where investors try to get their hands on every indicator available and combine them all, believing if they are all giving a 'buy' signal, 'it must be going up!' This is false. Using one indicator on a consistent basis may be just as effective as combining two, three, four or 100 indicators. Using 100 is simply more work. The second common mistake stems from the fact that no indicator works all the time. As a result, some investors and traders spend many hours, days, weeks and even years trying to develop the ultimate indicator that never gives a bad signal, or a signal that you never lose money with. Save yourself the time—no such indicator exists.

Instead, choose one indicator that works for you. In choosing an appropriate indicator, follow these steps:

1   Find something that you understand.

2   Learn how to use it properly and start using it consistently.

3   You will have losing trades; just try to keep them small.

4   Let your winning trades run.

5   Expect to have more losing trades than winning trades.

As already mentioned, if your winning trades are on average sufficiently bigger than your losing trades, over time you should be in front.

Using indicators

Let's look at one of the simplest indicators around today and the ways it can be traded. Following this, we will add a trigger to it to see if we can bring our timing down to a specific day and improve the efficiency of the filter or indicator.

The moving average

The moving average is a common tool familiar to many investors and traders. The moving average is an average of the closing prices for the last 'n' days. In the formula, 'n' equals the number of periods. So a 30-day moving average is therefore an average of the last 30 days' closing prices, rolled forward one day at a time. Similarly a three-day moving average is an average of the last three days, rolled forward one day at a time.

Table 14.1 may help illustrate how we calculate the (three-day) moving average.

Table 14.1: calculation of a moving average

Closing prices	Calculation	Moving average
$1.50		
$1.55		
$1.61	$1.50 + $1.55 + $1.61 /3	$1.55
$1.70	$1.55 + $1.61 + $1.70 /3	$1.62
$1.68	$1.61 + $1.70 + $1.68 /3	$1.66
$1.71	$1.70 + $1.68 + $1.71 /3	$1.69

All we are doing is adding up the total of the last 'n' period's closes and then dividing by 'n'. This gives us a series of numbers that we can plot as a line on a price chart. Figure 14.16 helps to illustrate what a moving average might look like.

Figure 14.16: example of a moving average

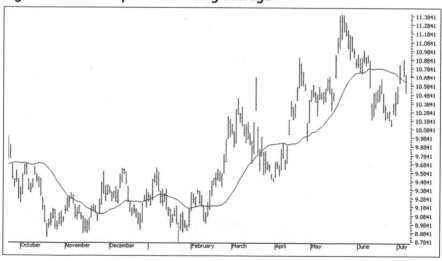

The first step in trading with a moving average is to decide how many days, weeks or months 'n' equals. The larger the number, the smoother the moving average will be. You will also have fewer trades and fewer false signals. The downside is that you will give away a lot of the move before getting in and before getting out. With a shorter term moving average, you will get into a trend earlier and exit closer to the top, but you will also have many trades and many false signals—and, therefore, more losing trades. Experiment to find out what works best for you by looking at, say, 15 days if you are a short-term trader, or 30 weeks if you are a long-term investor.

The common way to trade the moving average is to buy a share if its price breaks above its moving average and to sell it again when the price falls below the moving average. In figure 14.17 you can see that the price broke above the moving average around $27.00 and then traded higher, not breaking below the moving average again until the far right of the chart around the $31.00 mark.

Figure 14.17: moving averages during an uptrend and start of a downtrend

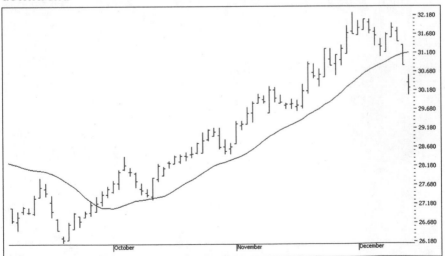

Applying the moving average

Before you go racing off to plot the moving average on every share and buy everything that rises above it, a few points are worth remembering. Nothing works all the time. As shown in figure 14.17, the moving average is an indicator that can keep you in an uptrend for a long time. It is also good as a signal to get out of the market during a downtrend as the price moves below the moving average, also shown in figure 14.17.

Once the price moves below the moving average, there is a risk that a downtrend could transpire. Because of this risk the trader may stand aside. If the downtrend continues, stepping aside will have prevented further losses.

In a non-trending market, however, the moving average will always see you lose money when traded in its classic fashion. In a sideways market such as that shown in figure 14.18, the moving average travels through the middle of the prices and forces the trader to buy high and sell low every time. This is a sure-fire way to lose money. So a moving average should only be applied to a trending market.

Figure 14.18: buy and sell signals using moving averages during a non-trending market

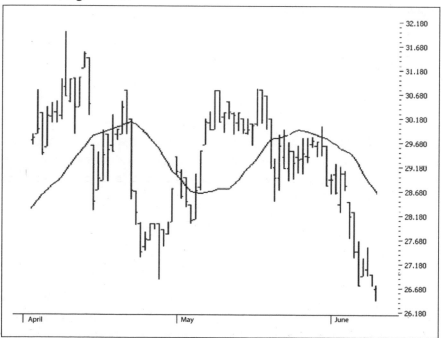

In a non-trending market, you can see that there would be a great deal of buying and selling activity on the part of the trader as the price crisscrosses above and below the moving average. Figure 14.18 illustrates this point and shows that the moving average needs to be used in conjunction with our earlier definition of an uptrend—that is, higher highs and higher lows.

While a ranging market can be traded, it is not through using trend-following indicators. Instead, we need to use tools known as oscillators, which are outside the scope of this book.

Combining tools

Earlier in this book, we discussed analysing companies using fundamental techniques such as ratio analysis. Suppose you came across two companies in a sector of the economy that was enjoying some growth. Now suppose you looked at the economic environment, and with low interest rates, inflation subdued and an expanding money supply you decided that the environment was ripe to make an investment in the sharemarket. Both growth companies display the following characteristics:

- low debt to equity
- high dividend yield
- strong return on equity
- strong historical dividend growth.

Let's also assume that the price for each share is exactly the same. The only difference between the two is that Company A's shares are above the moving average and Company B's shares are below a declining moving average. What would you do?

In this situation, all of the available fundamental information has been combined to find two companies that represent an opportunity. By adding technical analysis, you may discover that the market's consensus view (as reflected in the chart of each company's share price) for Company A appears better than that for Company B. Perhaps there is some information known in the market about Company A that you have not discovered. Alternatively, perhaps there is no other available information and the share price chart is illustrating the better market sentiment surrounding Company A's shares.

We may speculate about what is going on but the combination of fundamental analysis and technical analysis has provided us with a more complete picture than was available with just fundamental analysis.

Triggers

This is a possible third step in the technical analysis process. After defining the trend and adding a filter, a trader might utilise a trigger to fine-tune the entry. The moving average can be used as a trading tool; however, its effectiveness can sometimes be improved by combining it with a trading trigger. A trigger is a formation that must occur or a price level that must be breached before a trade is taken.

One method that has been used over many years is called the channel breakout method. Here the trader looks for a breakout above a previous period's highest high. Suppose we decided we would look for shares that have broken above their 30-day moving average. As a further confirmation, we would then only take the trade if in the next two days the price rises above the high of the day that broke above the moving average. The trigger works as another filter to confirm that the market is rising. Figure 14.19 may help explain this.

Figure 14.19: trading triggers using channel breakouts

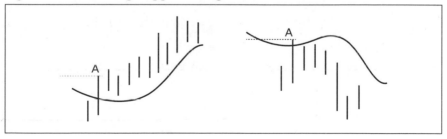

What we are attempting to do is to improve the moving average by requiring prices to not merely cross above the moving average but, after crossing above the moving average, to also break (within the next two days) the high of the day that first broke the moving average.

Look at the second diagram in figure 14.19. Notice that the price of the share rose above the moving average on the day marked 'A'. The price subsequently dropped below the moving average again before falling sharply. If we simply subscribed to the common method of trading a moving average, we would have bought at day A and been stuck with a share that was going down.

In the first diagram in figure 14.19, the day that broke the moving average is marked 'A' again. According to the traditional moving average approach, traders would buy on day A because prices crossed above the moving average line. By using the 'trigger' described above, we can avoid the mistake of buying simply because the price crossed the moving average once and then suffering for it if prices immediately dropped again, leaving us caught with a share that is still in its downtrend.

Have a look at the dashed line in the first diagram in figure 14.19. You will notice that the dashed line corresponds with the high of the day that broke above the moving average. The dashed line in the second diagram corresponds to the same event. There is a very big difference between the two diagrams. In the first, the price in the following two days stays above the dashed line. Within the next two days the price has risen above the high of the day that broke above the moving average. This can be taken as an indication that there is further strength in the market.

Look carefully at the second diagram and you will see that the price never rose above the high of the day that broke the moving average; therefore a trade was never triggered. Using the trigger in combination with the moving average saw the trader take the trade in the first diagram but not the trade in the second.

The use of a trigger may help you to avoid losing trades. In turn, this has the result of reducing not only the extent of losses in our trading account, but also the number of overall trades and the brokerage associated with those trades.

* * *

The reason why there are so many books written by finance experts is that people attach more credence to the words of those who have backed up their words with deeds. In the case of investing that means making money. In chapter 15 we will provide a quick introduction to some top fund managers.

Examples of investment strategies

In this chapter, we will set out the basic mechanics of six share selection strategies for you to consider in constructing your share portfolio.

The following share selection ideas by no means represent the best or even an exhaustive collection. The following techniques are simple models investors can investigate as a starting point to determine not only their effectiveness but also their suitability.

Before you implement your investment strategy, you should speak with your financial adviser and determine the approach's suitability for you given your needs and circumstances.

Strategy #1: Upside potential

Once you have established a universe of shares to consider, you can rank them in terms of their 'forecast' upside potential based on the current earnings per share (EPS) and forecast EPS growth rate. (EPS is the portion of profit earned for every share on issue. It shows at a glance the growth in earnings from one year to the next.)

The mechanics

Obtain the following for your target company:

¤   share price

¤   EPS

¤   EPS growth rate.

Subjectively determine a growth hurdle (GH)—for example, 8 per cent. Calculate a forecast share price by multiplying the EPS by the EPS growth rate. Now determine the rate of growth required to attain the forecast price. Finally, rank your universe by this rate to find those companies that are showing the greatest promise based on what the analysts believe are the companies' respective future earnings and expected growth rates.

In table 15.1 we look at two companies: company A and company B. The shares of both companies are trading at $1.10 and both are expected to earn 10¢ per share next year. This puts the shares for both companies on a prospective P/E ratio of 11 times next year's earnings. The two companies differ, however, when the rate of earnings growth is compared. Company A is expected to see earnings grow by 25 per cent to earn 10¢ per share next year, while company B is expected to see 15 per cent growth in earnings. Using the formula we described above (multiplying the growth rate by the forecast earnings per share) we find that company A may have greater upside potential.

Importantly, the formula we have used contains no hidden secrets to make it work. The resulting 'forecast' price is simply that—a forecast. There is no requirement for the shares to go to this price, so the forecast may prove to be incorrect. What we are doing here is ranking the shares in descending order, with those that have the greatest 'forecast' potential at the top, down to those that have the least upside potential or even a measured downside risk.

Table 15.1: calculating the potential upside

	Company A	Company B
Current price	$1.10	$1.10
Forecast EPS	$0.10	$0.10
EPS growth rate	25%	15%
Forecast price	$2.50	$1.50
Potential upside	127.27%	36.36%

But remember that before this technique is adopted a universe of shares must first be established. The method above then serves to rank those companies in order of your chosen merit system. Beyond this point, further research can be conducted into those companies that rank highly—say, the top 10 to 15 shares, or the top 10 to 20, could form the first portfolio. Remember to crosscheck your selections with an adviser to determine a particular share's suitability for your goals.

Strategy #2: Projected price range

This model is a variation on the theme above. It is simpler and will make more sense when you explain it to others such as your broker if you are utilising the services of a full-service adviser.

The mechanics

Select your investment universe—usually 50 to 100 companies. Establish the historical five-year P/E range for each share, or use any number of years that you prefer—the more the better. (P/E ratio or price/earnings ratio is the share price divided by the earnings per share. You can use this to determine for how many years you would need to own the shares before the funds you invested would be returned to you.) Calculate the average P/E for each share by adding the five-year P/E high and the five-year P/E low, then dividing the total by two. Establish next year's forecast EPS. (Forecast EPSs are usually included in analysts' reports, which are available from brokers or reported in the financial press. Market data subscription services are another option, and listed companies often provide access to analysts' reports on their websites too.) Multiply next year's forecast EPS by the average P/E to come up with next year's price target. Now rank the universe, with those currently trading the furthest below the forecast price target at the top of the list. The 10 to 20 shares at the top of the list may represent the most undervalued (relatively speaking) given their historical P/E ranges.

Let's look at an example to see the technique in operation. Imagine that shares in company A have traded at a P/E high of 17.75 times earnings and a P/E low of 6.69 times earnings. The average P/E for company A has therefore been 12.2; that is: $(17.75 + 6.69) \div 2$. The anticipated earnings per share for the coming year is 30¢ to 38¢ per share. After multiplying this by the average P/E of 12.2 times, we obtain a 'projected' price range for the shares of between $3.66 and $4.63. If the shares are trading within this range, this method suggests there is still some potential for the shares to rise. However, what we are ideally looking for is that both the lower and upper bands of next year's forecast price range are well above the current trading price.

It then becomes a matter of ranking companies by the greatest price gap between the current trading price and the lower end of the band.

Strategy #3: A longer term approach

The next strategy picks shares based on a longer term investment time frame using growth potential based on return on equity, debt to equity and dividend yield.

The mechanics

Select the investment universe. Select the top 25 by return on equity. Remove any company that has made a loss in the past 10 years. From the remaining companies, rank by debt to equity from lowest to highest debt-to-equity ratios. Remove the bottom half with the highest ratios. Now rank the remaining companies by dividend yield in descending order. The stocks at the top may represent the most out of favour and, as such, undervalued (relatively speaking), given the higher dividend yield.

Strategy #4: A medium-term approach

The fourth strategy picks shares based on a medium-term investment time frame using P/E ratios.

The mechanics

Take, for example, the top 100 industrial companies by market capitalisation. Rank them by P/E ratio in ascending order (lowest to highest). Isolate the top 30 (those 30 with the lowest P/Es). Own those securities with underlying businesses that have the following characteristics:

¤ current assets at least 1.5 times current liabilities

¤ debt less than 110 per cent of current assets

¤ no losses in the last five years

¤ a stable dividend record

¤ earnings this year higher than last year

¤ price less than 1.2 times net tangible assets.

Re-rank and re-weight at the end of 12 (or 24) months and repeat the process.

Strategy #5: A longer term approach using dividend yield

This strategy is again based on a long-term approach. The method for picking shares in this strategy is based on dividend yields.

The mechanics

Take, for example, the top 100 industrial companies by market capitalisation. Rank them by dividend yield from highest to lowest. Take the top 10 shares. Hold for 12 months. Re-rank and re-weight at the end of 12 months and repeat the process.

Strategy #6: A longer term approach using price/sales ratios

The final strategy is also based on a long-term time frame, this time using price/sales ratios.

The mechanics

Isolate the top 100 companies by market capitalisation. Rank them by price/sales per share. Isolate those with a price/sales ratio of less than 1. From this list, select the 10 companies with shares that have risen the most in the previous 12 months. Allocate equal dollar amounts to the 10 companies and then review and re-weight in 12 months' time.

* * *

Getting the picture? Ranking companies by their respective internal strengths and weaknesses, by the valuations imposed on their shares by the market, or by a combination of the two are valid methods of share selection for the purposes of portfolio construction.

Some of the strategies above were originally postulated by Benjamin Graham. The final strategy looks for companies that are still cheap but have had a good run in the market over the previous year. It recognises the idea that 'the trend is your friend' and that the strength in the share may be for reasons not widely known or understood in the market. This strategy is taking advantage of market 'inefficiency'.

They have all been tested, and the adherence to strategies such as these has seen individual years of good performance. And, as with any method, they have seen individual years of underperformance. While the past has been kind to these strategies, there is no guarantee that any will work in the future. The important message here is that you must develop a strategy of some description, one that is logical, cogent and internally consistent. Even more importantly, once it is developed, you must apply it consistently.

Investment gurus

Before we move on from strategies for long-term investing, we will consider some investing methodologies that historically successful fund managers have promoted. Every year new books come out written by investors who have been successful in particular markets for particular periods of time using particular strategies. Sometimes their approach is adopted by others and regarded as a classic strategy; with others their strategy may not become widely adopted.

It is useful to read these books, consider their approaches and compare them to your own.

We have included a few examples, starting with what is regarded as a classic text: Benjamin Graham's *Security Analysis: Principles and Techniques*.

Benjamin Graham

In 1934, Graham co-authored his book with colleague David Dodd. This book contained a lasting message—the rational investor does not play to market swings. Graham and Dodd described the market as a voting machine, not a weighing machine, and insisted that the market was often illogical. In 1949, Graham followed his original work with a second book, *The Intelligent Investor*. This book stressed the importance of developing a 'margin of safety'. Graham suggested that investors should look for large gaps between a share's worth and its price. It was this work that attracted the attention of Warren Buffett, who first enrolled in Graham's class at Columbia in 1950 and then applied to work for Graham at his funds management firm between 1954 and 1956.

Graham relied heavily on a quantitative (numbers) approach to evaluate businesses. Using the balance sheet and a number of numerical tests, Graham often found companies priced below net asset value. Graham often looked for businesses that displayed the following characteristics:

◻ debt/equity less than 50 per cent

◻ price/book less than 1.2

¤   current ratio greater than 2

¤   quick ratio greater than 1

¤   price/net working capital less than 1.

Essentially, if a business's shares were worth $1 and were selling for 40¢, Graham was interested. To be fair to modern-day investors, these criteria are very restrictive and you will find it difficult to find businesses that meet all of these criteria without following the markets every single day. Indeed, the criteria were so restrictive they led to Buffett considering the arguments put forward by another successful investor, Charlie Munger, and formulating his own approach before teaming up with Munger at Berkshire Hathaway. The general themes of Graham's theory, however, are still relevant to investors today. Throughout Graham's life, there were 14 investment philosophies he consistently espoused. They are summarised below:

1   Be an investor, not a speculator. Don't try to profit from market movements.

2   Question whether the company is worth its market capitalisation.

3   Apply the net current asset value (NCAV) rule. Find the NCAV by subtracting all of a firm's liabilities (including preferred shares) from current assets. Purchase shares that are below their NCAV per share level.

4   Determine the intrinsic value of a company's shares.

5   Regard corporate figures with suspicion. Be wary of manipulation of earnings through accounting changes.

6   Don't worry about precision. While you can never expect to be exact, an appropriate margin of safety should protect an investor.

7   Don't worry about the mathematics. You do not need maths beyond simple algebra.

8   Diversification rule #1: hold a minimum of 25 per cent in bonds and 25 per cent in ordinary shares.

9   Diversification rule #2: try to have at least 30 different holdings of equities.

10   When in doubt, stick to quality. Good earnings, solid dividend payout histories, low debt and reasonable P/Es are all signs of quality shares.

11   Use dividends as a sign. Risky growth shares seldom pay dividends. Look for companies that have treated their shareholders well and have a consistent and positive dividend policy.

12   Defend your shareholder rights. Complain if you feel management is not acting in shareholders' best interests.

13   Be patient. Be prepared financially and psychologically for poor results in the short term.

14   Think for yourself. Be independent and never stop thinking.

Peter Lynch

It's a while ago now, but from 1977 to 1990, Peter Lynch had a great run steering Fidelity Fund to a total return of 2510 per cent, or five times the 500 per cent return of the S&P 500 index. In his book, *One Up on Wall Street*, he described a variety of strategies that contributed to his success. These strategies divide attractive shares into different categories, each characterised by different criteria. Among those most easy to identify using quantitative research are fast growers, slow growers and stalwarts, with special criteria applied to cyclical and financial shares. Lynch's individual categories are outlined below.

Fast growers—combining growth with value

According to Peter Lynch, the characteristics of fast-growing companies are:

¤   they have little or no debt

¤   their earnings growth is 20 to 50 per cent a year

¤   their P/E ratio is below the company's earnings growth rate, meaning the PE to growth ratio is less than 1.

This approach is an interesting method because it combines growth with value. It seeks out those companies that show strong growth but are trading at the lowest prices relative to their earnings growth rates.

Slow growers—stocks for the tough times

The characteristics of slow-growing companies are:

¤ they are in the top quartile of sales revenue

¤ they have high dividend payout ratios

¤ they have sales that are growing faster than inventories

¤ they have a low yield-adjusted PE/G ratio.

Lynch argues you should invest in these companies for their premium income. They are often ignored during boom times, but investors will come flooding back when the first sign of a downturn is sniffed.

Stalwarts

The characteristics of stalwarts are:

¤ they have recorded positive earnings every year for the last five years

¤ they have a debt-to-equity ratio of 0.33 or less

¤ their sales growth rates are increasing in line with, or ahead of, inventories

¤ they have a low yield-adjusted PE/G ratio.

Generally, stalwarts have only moderate earnings growth but can have a potential for significant share price gains over the medium term if they can be purchased at attractive prices.

William O'Neil

William O'Neil became popular in the 1980s when he launched *Investor's Daily*, a business newspaper in the United States. Regarded as a growth and momentum investor, O'Neil pioneered data mining by computer. By studying the characteristics of the best 500 growth companies over the last 30 years, he developed a rigorous share selection discipline based on numerous fundamental and technical factors.

Common characteristics of O'Neil's target companies are as follows:

◻ they are industry leaders

◻ they have strong relative strength readings (indicating that they have performed very well relative to the overall market)

◻ they have recorded a perfect earnings record of substantial EPS increases over time

◻ they are poised to reach new highs following at least eight weeks of consolidation (trading within a range, while showing no definitive trend either up or down).

O'Neil's strategy is extremely aggressive and only appropriate for investors who are comfortable paying a premium for fast-growing companies. This is momentum investing in its purest form and harbours all of its dangers.

Martin Zweig

Martin Zweig used a long list of earnings criteria, including:

◻ quarterly earnings that are positive and growing faster than they were:

– a year ago

– in the preceding three quarters

– over the preceding three years

◻ annual earnings that are up for at least the past five years

◻ sales that are growing as fast as or faster than earnings, since cost-cutting and other non-revenue producing measures alone can't support earnings growth forever

◻ a P/E ratio of at least five — to weed out weak companies — but no more than three times the current market P/E or 43, whichever is lower.

James P O'Shaughnessy

James O'Shaughnessy set out his strategy in a book called *What Works on Wall Street*.

Based on his research, O'Shaughnessy developed two key investment strategies: 'cornerstone growth' and 'cornerstone value'.

The cornerstone growth strategy invests in companies with:

¤   a market capitalisation of at least $150 million (a different threshold level may be more appropriate for the Australian market)

¤   a price-to-sales ratio below 1.5

¤   persistent earnings growth

¤   performance results that are among the market's best over the prior 12 months.

This strategy makes sense for value-oriented growth investors who have the patience and personality to stick with a purely quantitative investment approach.

The cornerstone value strategy, on the other hand, invests in large companies with:

¤   strong sales

¤   strong cash flows

¤   the highest dividend yields.

* * *

Well done—you've made it! This is a great start to your journey and now you need to decide what to do next. You don't need to invest a lot with your first trade. At the start, it's all about getting started. Good luck!

Glossary

All Ordinaries Accumulation Index This index lists the same companies as the All Ords but also takes into account reinvesting dividends in calculating returns.

All Ordinaries index (All Ords) This index measures the level of share prices at any given time for approximately 500 of the largest Australian companies to determine the overall performance of the sharemarket. The index was established by the ASX at 500 points in January 1980. The companies are weighted according to their size in terms of market capitalisation (total market value of a company's shares).

annual report In the context of the Australian sharemarket, the annual report is a financial report or statement issued by a publicly listed company to its shareholders. The annual report contains a statement of financial performance, a statement of financial position and a statement of cash flow, as well as notice of the annual general meeting (AGM) and business resolutions to be discussed.

annuity A series of identical fixed payments to be made for a specified number of years.

ASIC (Australian Securities & Investments Commission) The government body responsible for (among other things) regulating companies, the issue and sale of shares and trust units, company borrowings, and investment advisers and dealers, in accordance with the *Corporations Act 2001* (Cth).

asset allocation The proportion of your total capital you invest in the different asset classes. This will be largely determined by your risk profile.

at limit An order that places a limit on either the highest price that may be paid for shares or the lowest price that may be accepted for sale.

at market An order that is placed at a price where the bid equals the best opposing offer, or the offer equals the best opposing bid. (This order type is superseded by 'market to limit'.)

bear market A market where share prices are falling and general sentiment is to expect further falls.

bid The price at which someone is prepared to buy shares (the opposite of offer).

blue chip Shares, usually highly valued, in a major company known for its ability to make profits in good times or in bad, with reduced risk of default.

bonus shares/bonus issue Additional shares issued by a company to existing shareholders for free, usually in a predetermined ratio to the number of shares already held.

bottom-up approach The investment process of selecting shares looking at individual companies: their outlook, what they do and their financial information.

brokerage A fee paid to a stockbroking firm for buying or selling of shares.

bull market A market where share prices are generally rising.

business cycle Also known as the 'economic cycle'. The rise and fall of the economy, from a peak, or boom, to a trough (sometimes called a depression) and back to a peak. The length and duration of each phase is not predictable.

capital Funding for investment in capital assets or to operate a business. Also refers to the value of an investment in a business or in assets such as property or shares.

capital growth An increase in the value in an asset such as an investment in shares. Capital growth is realised as a capital gain when the asset is sold for more than its purchase price.

cash management trust A fixed-interest trust designed specifically for short-term investors. This means entry and exit fees are not normally charged. Interest usually accrues on a daily basis at a variable rate related to the actual earning rate each day.

CHESS The ASX's Clearing House Electronic Sub-Register System, which provides the central register for the electronic transfer of share ownership.

company report Under the *Corporations Act 2001* (Cth), a listed company must provide a range of reports. These include half-yearly reports and preliminary final reports, as well as annual reports.

contract note (also known as a confirmation) A written document confirming a transaction between two dealers or a broker and a client that details the costs, type and quantity of shares traded.

contrarian investors Investors who invest against the general tide and sentiments of the market.

contributing shares Shares that have been partly paid for. At a future date the shareholder will be required to pay the balance outstanding, unless the company is a no liability company in which case shares can be forfeited instead.

convertible note A loan made to a company at a fixed rate of interest with the right to be either redeemed (that is, repaid by the company) for cash or converted into ordinary shares at a predetermined date or within a certain period.

cum dividend Cum means 'with'. Shares quoted cum dividend entitle the buyer to the current dividend. The price of the shares will usually reflect the amount of the dividend. Similarly, shares 'cum rights' enable the buyer to participate in the new issue of shares.

cyclicals Businesses that are reliant on the general economy for growth and have little intrinsic protection against soft periods.

debenture A loan to a company at a fixed rate of interest and for a fixed term, usually one to five years. The debenture is secured by a trust deed over an asset, or assets, of a company.

derivatives Derivatives are instruments that derive their value from that of underlying instruments (such as shares, share price indices, fixed-interest securities, commodities and currencies). Warrants and exchange-traded options are types of derivatives.

diversification Spreading investments over a variety of investment categories in order to reduce risk. You may also invest in different countries to spread your risk.

dividend Distribution to shareholders. Usually expressed as a number of cents per share.

dividend cover A ratio showing the number of times a company's dividend is covered by its net profit. Dividend cover ratio equals net profit divided by total dividend paid. A low dividend cover points to a company paying out most of its net profit, while a high cover suggests much of the profit is being retained.

dividend imputation The tax credits passed on to a shareholder who receives a franked dividend. Under provisions of the *Income Tax Assessment Act*, imputation credits entitle investors to a rebate for tax already paid by an Australian company.

dividend per share (DPS) Represents the cash payment or distribution made by a company to shareholders on a per share basis. The payment is made out of the earnings of the company. Calculated by adding the interim dividend to the final dividend, DPS is usually expressed as cents per share.

dividend yield The annual dividend shown as a percentage of the last sale price for the shares. A simplified rate of return on an investment.

earnings per share (EPS) Measures the earnings that are attributed to each equivalent ordinary share over a 12-month period. It is calculated by dividing the company's earnings by the number of shares on issue.

equity capital or equity funding Capital raised by a company through issuing shares. An alternative to debt funding.

ex date The date at which a previously announced dividend or issue is deemed to take place. If you purchase shares on or after the ex date, you will not be entitled to the current new issue of shares or the dividend. You must purchase shares before the ex-dividend date to be entitled to that dividend.

ex dividend The ex-dividend date occurs two business days before the company's Record Date. To be entitled to a dividend a shareholder must have purchased the shares before the ex-dividend date. If you purchase shares on or after that date, the previous owner of the shares (and not you) is entitled to the dividend. A company's share price may move up as the ex-dividend date approaches and then fall after the ex-dividend date.

fixed asset An asset that is not easily converted into cash, such as your house or superannuation.

float The initial raising of capital by public subscription to securities, such as shares offered on the sharemarket for the first time.

franked dividend A dividend paid by a company out of profits on which the company has already paid tax. The investor is entitled to an imputation credit, or reduction in the amount of income tax that must be paid, up to the amount of tax already paid by the company.

fundamental analysis A method of analysis using ratios and percentages calculated from financial data of a company to assess the company's quantitative and qualitative aspects. Ratios of particular industry groups and/or major competitors may also be included in the analysis to determine its suitability for investment.

general market risk The risk of volatility within the market as a whole or within a particular sector of the market; for example, mining shares are usually more volatile than bank shares.

goods and services tax (GST) A broad-based tax on most supplies of goods and services consumed in Australia.

government bond A debt security issued by the government. Interest is usually paid twice yearly at a fixed rate for the life of the bond, which is usually 10 years.

growth companies Companies that have already achieved above-average earnings growth and are expected to continue doing so.

holder identification number (HIN) A number allocated by your stockbroking firm when you buy shares if you nominate the firm as your sponsor in CHESS.

income An investor's income includes dividends, interest and other payments received from investments. It does not include capital growth.

investment clock An analysis tool that sets out simply the economic and investment cycles using the analogy of a sweeping hour hand to pass through various economic stages or cycles.

liquid asset An asset that you can easily convert into cash, such as shares or fixed-interest investments.

liquidity Being able to convert assets into cash easily, quickly and with little or no loss of capital. A liquid market is a market with enough participants to make buying and selling easy.

listed company A company that has agreed to abide by the ASX Listing Rules so that its shares can be bought and sold on the ASX.

macroeconomic models Analysis methods that use economic data as inputs to forecast market movements.

margin call Occurs when the amount borrowed to invest in shares exceeds the lending margin. For example, a company agrees to lend money using shares as collateral to the value of 70 per cent of the shares. If the share price falls, the amount borrowed rises above 70 per cent and the borrower will be required to provide extra funds to bring the loan amount back to 70 per cent of the collateral.

market capitalisation The total number of shares on issue multiplied by their market price. This can be applied to work out the market value of one company or the value of all companies listed on the exchange.

market price The prevailing price of shares traded on the ASX. It may be the last price at which the shares traded, or the most recent price offered or bid for the shares.

negative gearing Negative gearing is a situation where you borrow money to invest in an income-producing asset and the income received from that asset is less than the interest expense. The interest expense on borrowed funds may be tax deductible.

net tangible assets (NTA) An indication of what each share in a company would be worth if all the assets were liquidated, all the debts were paid and the residual was distributed to the ordinary shareholders on a per share basis.

offer The price at which someone is prepared to sell shares (the opposite of bid).

off-market transfer The transfer of shares between parties without using a stockbroking firm as the intermediary. Off-market transfers are executed through the use of an Australian standard transfer form.

ordinary shares The most commonly traded security in Australia. Holders of ordinary shares are part-owners of a company and may receive payments in cash, called dividends, if the company trades profitably. A class of shares that has no preferential rights to either dividends out of profits or capital on a winding up.

preference shares Shares that rank before ordinary shares in the event of liquidation of the issuing company and that usually receive a fixed rate of return.

price/earnings ratio Shows the number of times the price covers the earnings per share over a 12-month period. Investors commonly use this ratio to measure the attractiveness of particular shares and to compare shares in one company with those in another.

price range for day The highest and lowest price at which a share traded over the course of a day.

prospectus The document issued by a company or fund setting out the terms of its public equity issue or debt raising. This provides the background and financial and management status of the company or fund, subject to the requirements of ASX Listing Rules and the *Corporations Act 2001* (Cth).

return/return on investment What you earn from your investments, including dividends, interest or other income and realised capital gains. Return is usually expressed as a percentage of the amount invested.

rights issue A privilege granted to shareholders to buy new shares in the same company, usually below the prevailing market price.

risk profile Your attitude to risk, determined by a range of factors including your stage of life, the amount you have to invest, your experience and confidence as well as your investment time frame.

S&P/ASX indices These measure the movement in share values resulting from trading on the ASX. The indices are constructed and calculated by Standard & Poor's.

securities A general term applied to all shares, debentures, notes, bills, government and semi-government bonds.

Security Holder Reference number (SRN) This is allocated by an issuer to identify a holder on an issuer-sponsored or certificated sub-register.

self-managed superannuation fund (SMSF) A super fund controlled by its trustees and regulated by the ATO. SMSFs can have no more than four members and must be run for the sole purpose of providing death or retirement benefits for the members or the members' dependants.

shares Shares represent part-ownership in a company. They can be ordinary shares, preference shares or partly paid (contributing) shares.

small-capitalisation shares / Small Ordinaries Index (XSO) The S&P/ASX Small Ordinaries Index is comprised of companies included in the S&P/ASX 300 index, but not in the S&P/ASX 100 index. This index provides a benchmark for small-cap investments (also called 'small-cap' stocks).

specific risk The risk of a particular share underperforming the market.

stockbroker Stockbrokers have direct access to the market for trading shares. Therefore, they can act as agents for buying or selling shares, for which a fee is charged. A broker may also offer a range of other products and services including providing advice on which shares to buy or sell.

technical analysis A method used to identify investment opportunities through the study of price action. A chart, representing past price movements, is the principal tool used to identify trends on which analysts can base their predictions.

top-down approach An investment philosophy that looks firstly at the social, economic and political forces that may affect the nature and shape of the economic cycle. From these theoretical positions, analysts examine and interpret market forecasts to develop a picture of the investment environment, which helps to determine whether the investment strategy should be bullish, bearish or neutral.

underwriter Guarantees to the company that the funds sought — through a float, for example — will be raised, that any shortfall will be taken up by the underwriter and that the funds will be available at a specific time.

unsecured notes A loan made to a company for a fixed period of time at a fixed rate of interest. They are issued mainly, but not only, by finance companies for between three months and three years. They offer a higher rate of interest than a debenture of the same maturity, but do not have the same security as a debenture.

volatility The measurement of the amount of fluctuation in price of the underlying security calculated using the standard deviation of average daily price change.

Index